Paper Fold Creations

Holidays and Seasons

Written and Created by
Delia A. Lefebvre

Published by CreateSpace
CreateSpace is a DBA of On-Demand Publishing LLC, part of the Amazon group.

for Maddie

Holidays and Seasons
Table of Contents

INTRODUCTION

This second book in the Paper Fold Creations series includes characters for holidays and seasons. Again, many of these characters have been made with classrooms of children and the end product is simply amazing. What wonderful memories these characters have created for students and families! Now, you can begin to create some of these same moments with your own children or students.

In the fall, there were always scarecrows hanging from my classroom ceiling that got many "Oohs" and "Aahs" from parents and passersby. The turkeys were always requested by families that knew about them from years past because they made a wonderful Thanksgiving centerpiece. To this day, even though their children are grown with children of their own, I have had parents tell me that they still pull out the Turkey as part of their holiday celebration.

The winter months brought snowmen decorated in various colored scarves and hats, sometimes embellished with mittens and fleece caps. Living in the Northeast Kingdom of Vermont, it was always interesting to try to find sticks for the arms in three or four feet of snow.

The Witch is a new creation made especially for this book, as is the Santa. I believe, however, that should you choose to make these with children, you will find the patterns, pictures and directions easy to follow. The bunny in this book was made and enjoyed by many smiling children as they looked forward to the snow melting and the holiday to arrive. May you bring that joy back to many more little ones.

As always, take your time to make many Chompers. This is the main piece of all of these characters and, once you are comfortable and confident in making this, then you can easily make any of these characters for yourself or with children. The two most challenging parts of any of these characters are making the Chomper and attaching the head to the body. Just practice and you'll do fine. Also, please be sure to visit my website at:

http://paperfoldcreations.wix.com/reations

This site gives you step-by-step video directions for making the Chomper as well as attaching the body to the head.

Helpful Tips Before You Begin

PAPER

Maybe the most important tip to follow when making these characters is to use a quality paper. I use the *Tru-Ray* brand of paper, which comes in a multitude of colors and is light enough to fold easily but heavy enough that it does not tear. It is not a *fibrous* construction paper and can be used in a photo copier...which is great when getting pattern pieces ready for a large group.

Most of the construction paper that you can purchase in local stores (they typically come in pads or assorted packs) is not the best to use for these projects, especially with children. It is difficult to get crisp folds with this paper and it tears easily...which can be very frustrating.

GLUE

Regardless of whether you are making these characters for yourself or with a group of children, having glue that cooperates is key. You do not want to sit and hold pieces for long periods of time or have pieces falling off that don't seem to want to stick. Have paper clips on hand to hold pieces together so you do not need to wait for the glue to set before moving onto the next step.

While there are many different kinds of glue on the market, and I have tried many of them, I have found that Tacky Glue works the best. It is thicker, sticks better and dries faster than most school glues.

Hot glue is also an option if you are looking to attach things quickly. It works well for quickly adding things like feathers, cotton balls, pompoms, google eyes, yarn, etc. I would not, however, recommend it when making and gluing the paper pieces of your character. Also, do not allow children access to the hot glue...Tacky Glue works just as well to attach all of these things it just takes a little longer to set.

MARKERS

These characters call for very little to be done in marker. The main thing that you will use marker for is adding detail to the characters and to make the centers of the eyes. For these, I recommend that you have one ultra fine point marker and one fine point.

I tend to use only black, but you can certainly vary the colors that you use for your own creations. I also do not use any type of water based marker when making the characters for myself because I do not want the marker to run...and anything from wet fingers to glue touching the marker will make that happen.

Permanent is the only way to go when making them for your own use. When making the characters with children, I typically use water-based markers. Permanent marker can have quite an odor and doesn't come off of little fingers so well.

OTHER TIPS

* Use a good pair of scissors. It will save you a lot of frustration in the long run.
* Plan ahead ... have what you need to make your character readily available.
* Have a large, clear, well-lit workspace. You'll want plenty of room to spread out.
* Try to have a variety of craft items on hand to add your own creative twist to your characters.
* Give yourself time to practice before attempting to make any of these characters with children.
* Have some light string or fishing line on hand to hang your characters.

If you have other Paper Fold Creations Books, you will find that some of the directions are replicated from one book to the next. This is ,simply, because all of these characters are built with the same set of folds that create "The Chomper" and the body parts are all attached in the same way. The differences will be found in the pattern pieces, color choices and in how pieces are attached that allow you to make a unique character each and every time.

*OTHER HELPFUL TIPS CAN BE FOUND ON PAGES 21, 33, 49, 65, 83 AND 99

Directions for "The Chomper"

Placing the paper *horizontally* in front of you, begin by folding your paper in half. It is important to have crisp, even folds.

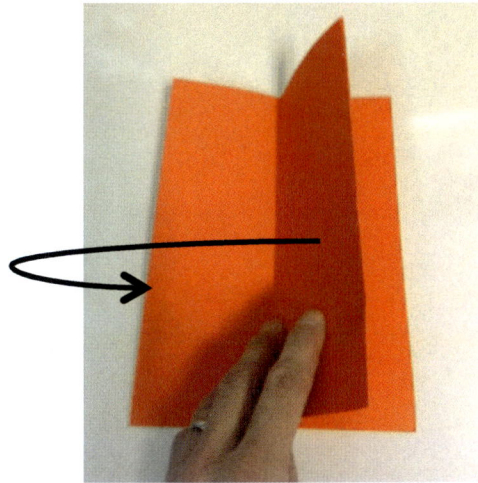

Fold the paper back so the side edge is even with the back fold.

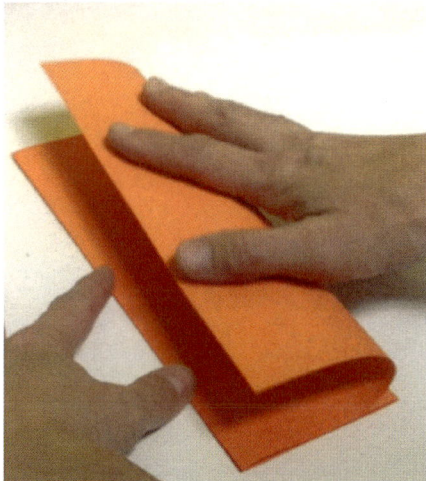

Flip the whole paper over and do the same thing to the back.

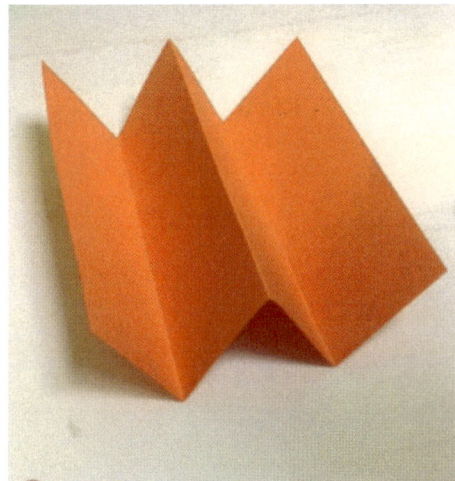

Open the paper and set it in front of you so it is in the shape of a "W".

Pinch the *centerfold* together.

Lay the centerfold down flat on the table.

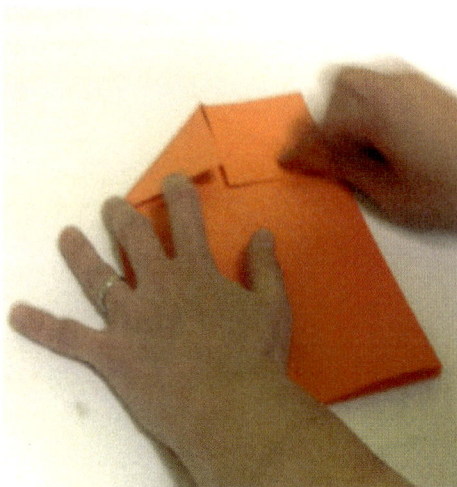

Take the top corner of the center fold and fold it in. The top edge of the folded corner should line up with the crease.

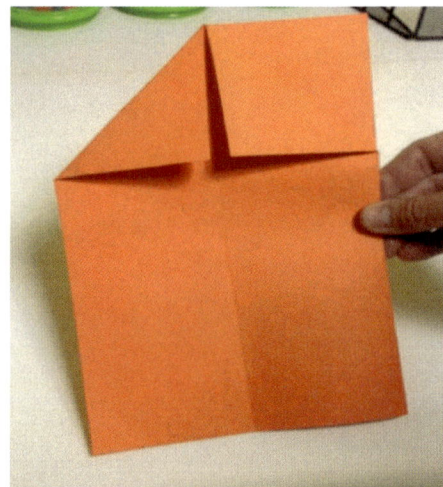

Do the same with the top corner of the other side. When you lay the paper in front of you, it looks like a house with a chimney.

Rotate the paper **180 degrees** so your "house is upside down". Follow the same directions from step 8 so your paper looks like this.

Fold the center to the right so it lays flat on top of the other corner folds.

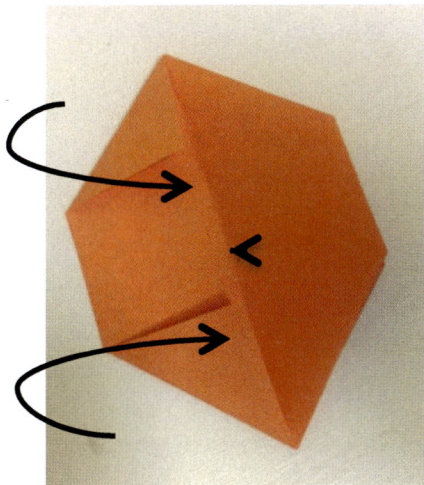

On the square edge, fold the corners of both top and bottom in to be even with the crease, making a **hexagon.**

➤ **If you have an opening at the crease, flip the paper over.**

Holding onto the corner folds you just created, fold the hexagon in half to create a **trapezoid**.

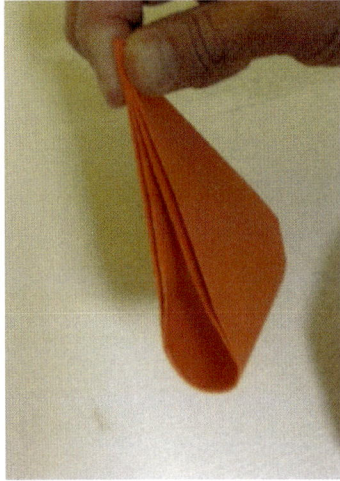

Fold the trapezoid in half to create a crease to mark the center. Lay the trapezoid flat in front of you.

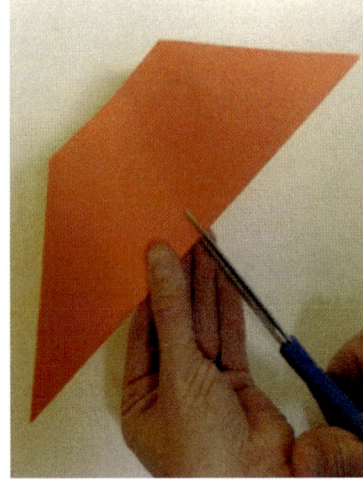

On the long edge of the trapezoid, snip about ½ inch into the center crease.

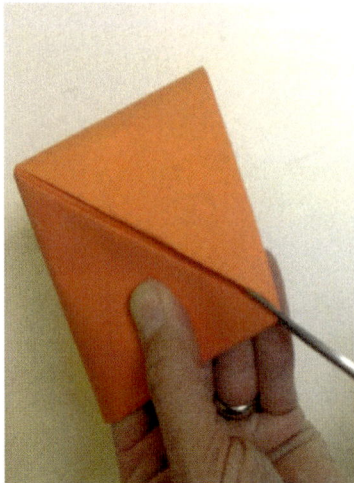

Slide your fingers into the opening on the long edge of the trapezoid to slightly open it. Snip about ½ inch into the end fold of the trapezoid. Do the same to the other end.

Lay the trapezoid flat. Fold the edges of the trapezoid back about a ½ inch, using the snips you created to guide your fold. Flip the trapezoid over and do the same to the other side.

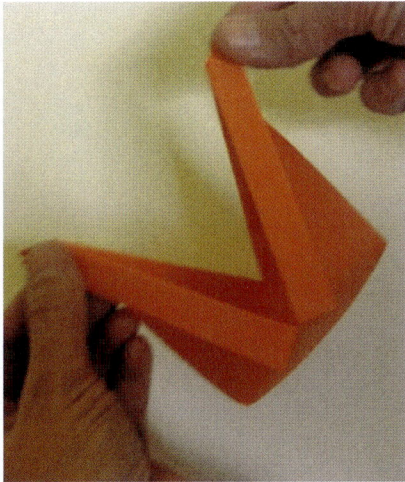
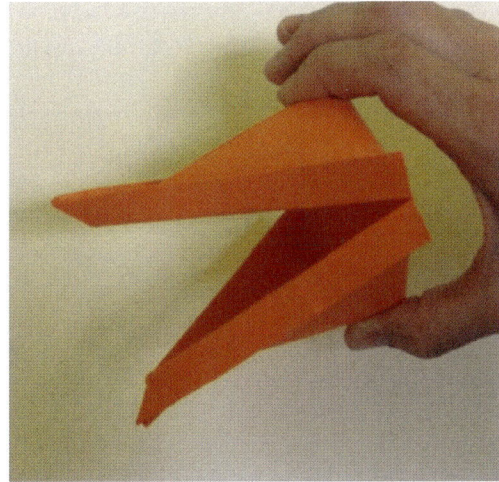

Put your hand in the opening on the long side of the trapezoid to open it up, bringing the points together. This is your completed Chomper and will be used to make the heads and bodies of the figures.

MAKING THE BODY

To make the body, you will need two Chompers. Take one of them and put glue around all four "lips" of only one of the Chompers.

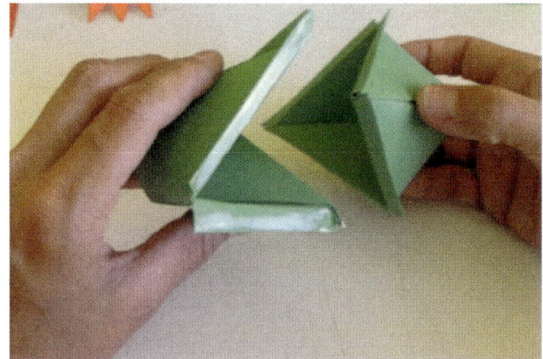

With one Chomper held open in one hand and the other Chomper held open in the other, bring the two pieces together as shown in the picture.

It can be difficult to do this step alone...it sometimes helps to have another set of hands to help.

Once the pieces are brought together, pinch the four "lips" of both Chompers together, running your fingers up and down the glued pieces until they stay together. You can also hold the pieces together by placing a paper clip on each of the four lips. This is the completed body.

ATTACHING THE HEAD AND BODY

Fold the two connector pieces in half, making an "L" shape. Put glue on the inside of the "L".

Slide the glued piece into the *seam* on the bottom of the head, sliding and keeping the "L" folded to the left seam on the head.

Follow the same steps with the second *connector piece* but, this time, slide the glued piece into the right side of the seam.

Apply glue to both tabs on the head.

ATTACHING THE HEAD AND BODY Continued

Holding onto the two tabs, gently pull them apart as you place them onto the top of the body. The head will be wobbly if you do not pull the tab far enough apart. This is another step that, while possible to do on your own, it often helps to have another set of hands to hold the body upright while you glue the head on.

Attaching the Arms and Legs

For the arm, put a small amount of glue on the end of the shorter strip of paper. Glue the hand to the strip of paper.

Put a small amount of glue on the other end of the strip. Find the side seam of the body and glue the arm inside the seam. Do the same for the other arm.

ALWAYS BEND THE ARMS FORWARD AT THE ELBOWS AND THE LEGS BACK AT THE KNEES TO GIVE YOUR CHARACTER SOME 'LIFE' AND TO MAKE IT LOOK LESS STIFF.

Snip ½" into the end of each leg piece (longer strips). Fold one tab to the right and one tab to the left, as shown in the picture. Put glue onto both tabs and glue onto the foot , placing it near the back/heel.

Apply glue to the top of the legs. Insert them into the bottom seam of the body, pressing the glued piece to the inside of the body seam. Placement of the legs is up to you...I prefer to have them spread out a bit rather than straight up and down

MAKING HAIR

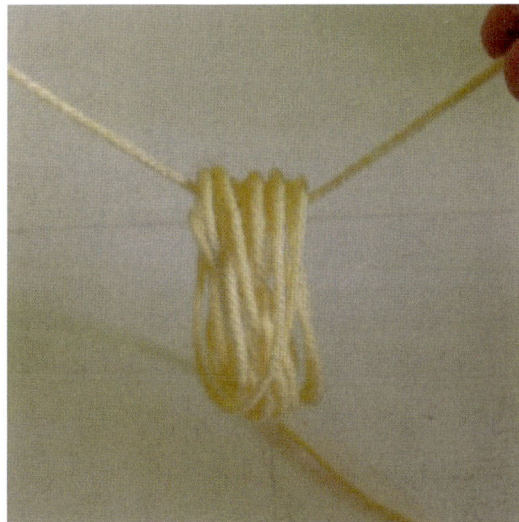

Wrap string or yarn around your fingers about ten times and snip the end. The more that you spread your fingers, the longer the hair will be.

Remove the string from your fingers. Thread another piece of string (about 6 inches) through the loops.

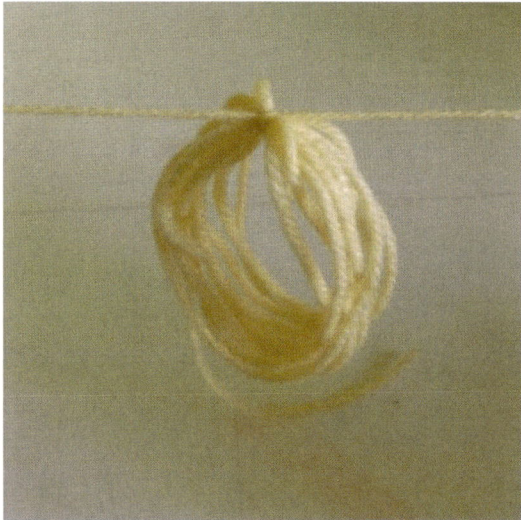

Tie the string that you just looped through into a knot. Let the string hang down to become a part of the loops.

Tie another piece of string (about six inches) around all of the looped string, just below the knot. This will create a 'ball' at the top.

Holding onto the ball of string, snip the ends of the loop to the desired length.

This is a completed 'clump' of hair. Use different colors and different lengths to add personality to your characters.

The Scarecrow

The Scarecrow

MATERIALS

	Color	Paper
Body (2 chompers)	Blue	6" X 9"
Head (2 chompers)	Tan or Flesh	4 1/2" X 6"
Arms / Legs (x2)	Blue / Green	Use pattern
Hat Pieces (x1 each)	Brown	Use pattern
Eyes (x2)	Outside white / inside black	Use pattern
Hands (x2)	Tan or Flesh	Use pattern
Shoes (x2)	Dark Brown or Black	Use pattern
Yarn	gold or yellow	Follow directions on pgs 17-18
Other Materials	Tacky Glue, scissors, black permanent marker	butons, fabric scraps for patches, orange pompom for nose

Getting Started

Begin by getting all of your pieces traced, cut and folded. Use the directions for 'The Chomper' to make the head and the body parts.

Pattern pieces for the rest of the character you are building are included in the back of the book on **PAGES 108-111.**

I recommend making copies of ALL PATTERN PIECES from the book to use in making your characters rather than cutting the pieces from the book itself. To do this, trace using light paper or tracing paper or copy them on a photo copier.

There are a few ways to cut the pattern pieces:

- For a large group, use a quality paper and make copies from the template using a copy machine. OR...

- Place the included pattern page on top of the colored paper you will be using and cut them out at the same time. This will only allow you to use the pattern one time unless you copy it on a copier first. OR...

- Place the included pattern page on top of a piece of heavy *tag board*. Cut the pattern and tag board at the same time to create heavy pattern pieces that can be traced and used over again. Store the pieces in a labeled envelope.

* **When you need two or more of something (hands, feet, eyes, head/body connectors, etc.) it is recommended that you fold your paper in half, or more, so you are cutting all pieces out at the same time.**

One adaptation that can be made for The Scarecrow is to make the head out of two tan Chompers rather than from a circle cut from a paper bag. Both versions are super cute and there is not really any difference in how the the pieces go together. Use the same pattern pieces to make either one.

Using the pattern for the head, cut a circle out of paper bag. Crumple a sheet of paper towel into a ball.

Wrap the paper circle around the ball of paper towel and tie at the bottom with a piece of yarn. This is the head.

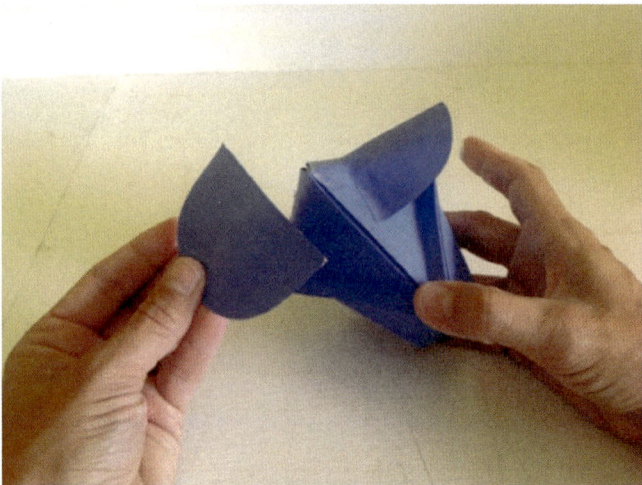

Make the body using the directions on **PAGES 9-14.** Apply glue along the flat edge of the shoulder pieces. Wrap the glued edged over each shoulder as shown, making sure that the body seam in in the front.

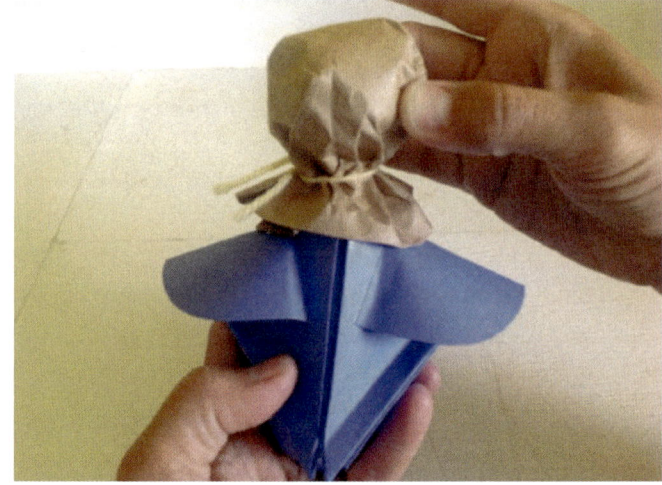

Smooth out a side of the head as well as you can for the face. Put glue inside the 'neck' and spread the paper bag out across the shoulder to glue down. Choose the best side to be the front of the Scarecrow.

MAKING AND ATTACHING THE ARMS

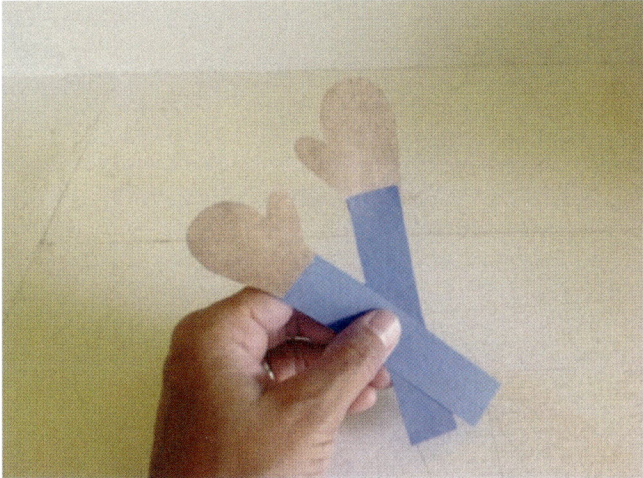

Glue the hands onto the arms. Make sure sure that you have both a left and a right arm.

Apply glue along one side edge of the trapezoid piece for the *cuff* of the sleeve. Wrap the trapezoid around the arm with the fatter part toward the elbow. The 'point' of the cuff points away from the thumb.

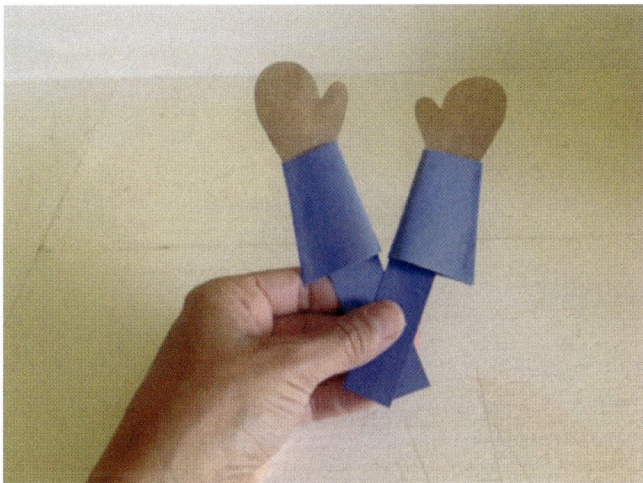

Here are the completed arms. Again, be sure that your thumbs are positioned so you have both a right and a left arm.

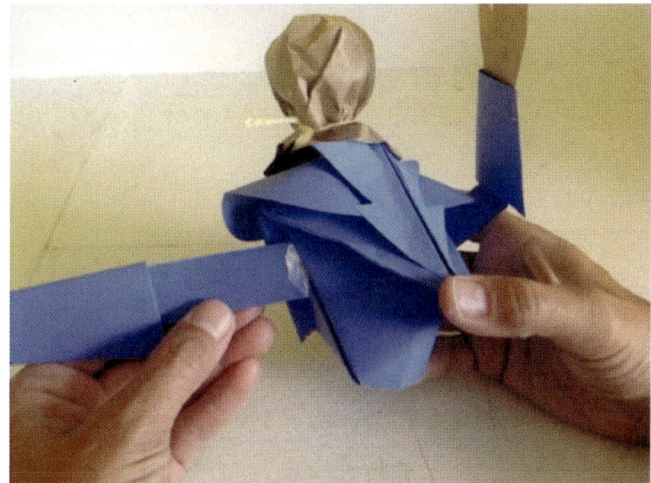

Use the directions on **PAGE 16** for attaching the arms.

Fold down the long edges of the rectangle about 1/2". Make small snips along both edges, snipping in as far as the fold that you made. The snips should be about 1/2" apart. This allows the paper to curl more easily and creates tabs to glue on the hat's top and bottom.

Apply glue along one short edge of the rectangle. Roll the rectangle into a tube and hold until the glue sets.

Fold all of the tabs of the tube inward. Apply glue to the tabs on one end, making sure to get glue right out to the edges.

Cut out the circle for the hat and center it onto the tube that you just made.

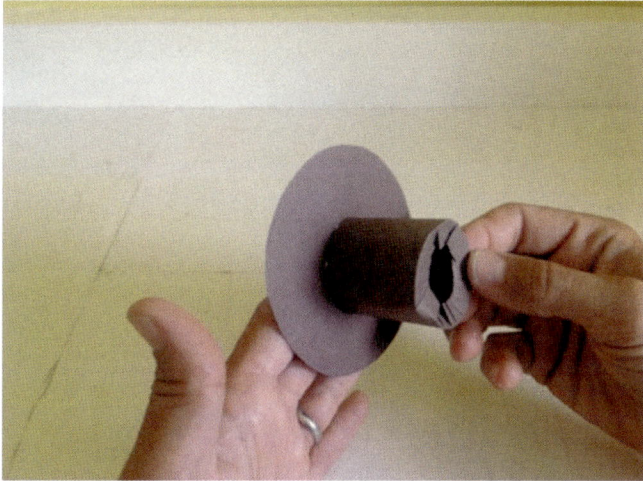

Hold/press the circle firmly to the tube and the tabs until it is secure. You may want to put your finger into the hat and press the tabs down from the inside.

Apply glue to the tabs on the top of the hat. For the top, you will use the square pattern piece and glue onto the tabs the same way that you did for the bottom.

Again, hold/press firmly in place until the glue has set. Be sure that the glue is fairly dry before using your scissors to trim away the extra. It helps to view the hat from below as you trim so you can see the tube as you cut.

Using a black, permanent marker, *cross-hatch* lines on the top, sides and rim of the hat to make it look like it is a straw hat.

Snip all around the rim of the hat, about 1/4" apart, cutting from the edge of the rim right back to the tube of the hat. This will help to make more of a straw appearance as well.

Gently crinkle the 'straw' rim and squeeze the hat to make it look old and worn.

Apply glue to the bottom of the hat and press firmly to the Scarecrow's head. You will need to hold it in place for a bit so it doesn't fall off.

MAKING AND ADDING HAIR

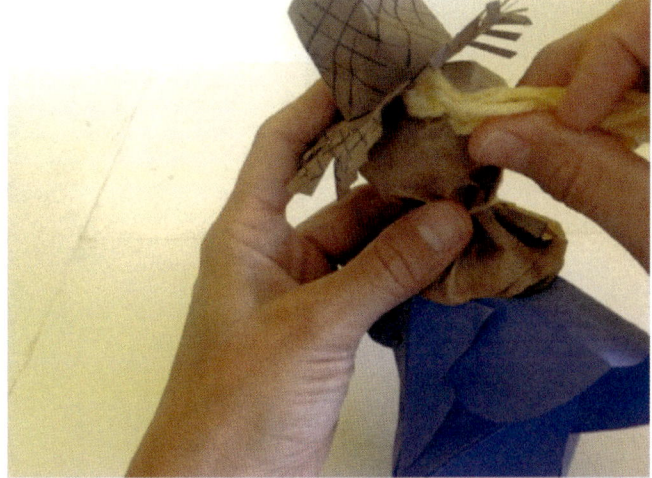

Use the directions on **PAGES 17-18** for making hair. Make about eight clumps of hair. How closely you glue them together will determine the exact number that you will need.

With children, the hair can be put on using Tacky Glue, but it does take patience on their part. I often have them make hair out of yellow paper to eliminate this issue (see directions on **PAGE 33**) When making my own, I use a hot glue gun.

Cut out the *lapel* for the jacket and glue to the center seam.

Cut out the tail pieces for the jacket and glue them to the Scarecrow's back, just below the 'v' on his body.

Make a few more clumps of 'hair' to use as the straw for the Scarecrow's arms and legs. Put some glue on the ball of the clump and insert it into the end of the sleeve.

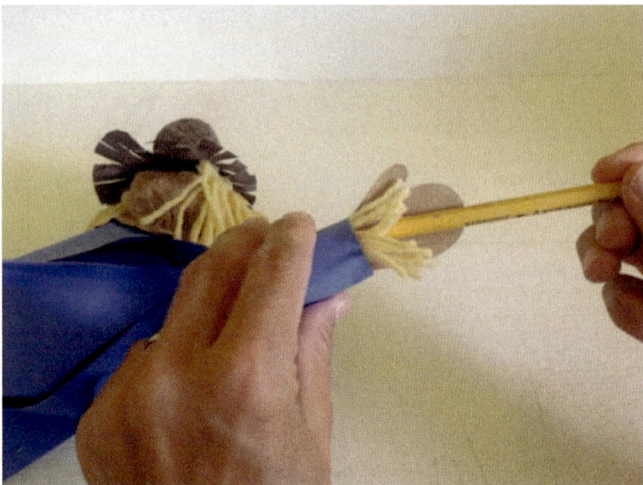

Use a pencil to push the 'straw' in as far as you like. You can put a clump on each side of his hand if you wish.

Decide how far you want the straw to stick out. If you need to, simply trim it to the desired length.

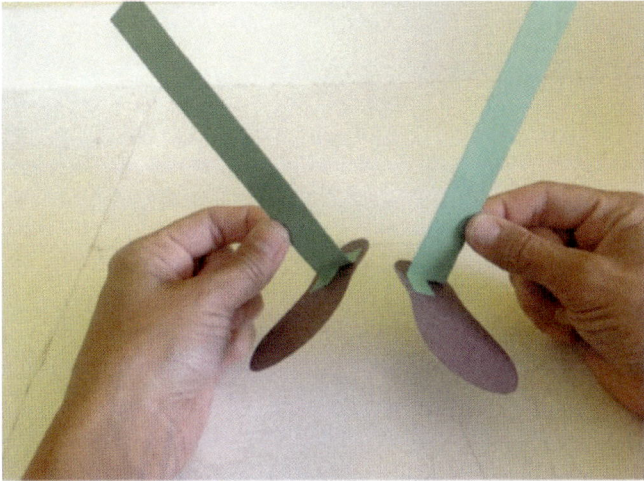

Use the directions on **PAGE 17** for attaching the legs and the feet.

Glue a clump of straw to the front of the Scarecrow's leg, allowing it to hang over his shoe as far as you like. If you would like the straw to go all the way around his leg, glue another clump to the back.

Just as with the arm, place some glue along the side edge of the trapezoid used for his leg. Wrap the trapezoid around the leg with the fat part on the bottom near the shoe.

Bend the legs at the knee to help to hold the pant bottoms in place and to give your scarecrow character. The pointed part of the leg bottom will point to the outside when you glue the leg to the body (see **PAGE 17**).

Glue on the eyes, nose, mouth, buttons and patches of fabric to complete your scarecrow.

He's all finished!

An alternative to making a paper bag head is to use two tan Chompers and glue them together as done with the Witch, Santa, Snowman and Bunny. Use the same size paper that is used to make the head for all of the characters. When attaching the hat, you will need to cut an 'x' in the bottom (as done with the Witch's hat on page 36) in order for it to stay on the head.

The Witch

THE WITCH

MATERIALS

	Color	Paper
Body (2 chompers)	Black	6" X 9"
Head (2 chompers)	Green	4 1/2" X 6"
Arms / Legs (x2) **Lips, Mouth, Teeth (x1)**	Black/ White Red	Use patterns/ Make your own
Hat Pieces (x1 each)	Black	Use pattern
Eyes (x2)	Outside white / inside black	Use patterns
Nose (x1), Hands (x2)	Green	Use patterns
Dress (x12), Shoes (x2)	Black	Use patterns
Yarn	Blue or Purple	
Other Materials	Tacky Glue, scissors, black permanent marker	buttons, colored or *foil paper* for hat strip, red marker

GETTING STARTED

Begin by getting all of your pieces traced, cut and folded. Use the directions for 'The Chomper' on **PAGES 9-15** to make the head and body parts.

Pattern pieces for the rest of your character are included in the back of the book on **PAGES 112-114.**

The Witch is a new creation made for this book and has never been made with children. This character is a little bit more involved than others so, if you decide to make her with children, plan on making some modifications to make it easier.

SUGGESTIONS FOR MODIFICATIONS

Make the body, head and hat as you would all of the other characters. When you get to the shoes and arms, use the same pattern pieces but use the directions on **PAGES 16-17.**

Make the hair out of paper. Using rectangular pieces of paper the length that you would like the hair to be, cut slits up the rectangle going almost all the way to the top. Don't cut all of the way through or you will have a lot of little separate strips to glue on. Use as many rectangles of hair as you need to get around the head and to overlap each other if you wish. Curl or crinkle the hair so it doesn't lay flat.

You can use the same pieces for the skirt and let children just glue them around the waist. Eliminate the directions that help the skirt to "puff" outward.

Make the head of the witch with green and the body with black, using the directions on **PAGES 9-15**.

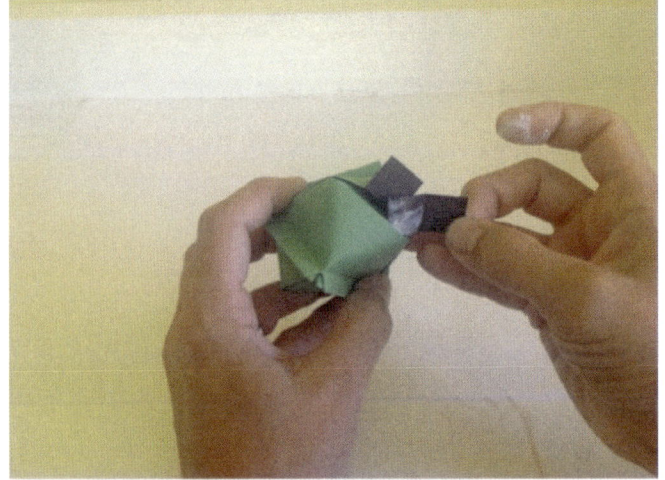

Use black tabs to connect the head to the body as seen on **PAGE 15.**

The black tabs allow them to blend in with the body.

Attach the head to the body using the directions on **PAGE 16**.

Cut the strip for the hat using the pattern piece and your choice of paper. Glue to the hat piece as shown.

Apply glue along half of the straight edge of the hat.

Bend the corner of the hat toward the center and wrap the glued edge around to create a *cone*. Before attaching, line up the colored strip as you bring the glued side around

This will be the top of the witch's hat.

Make small snips about 1/4" apart all the way around the bottom of the hat, snipping in as far as the colored strip.

Fold all of the tabs toward the center. Apply glue to the tabs, making sure that you get all the way out to the edges.

Firmly press the cone to the center of the circle rim for the hat. Hold until glue sets.

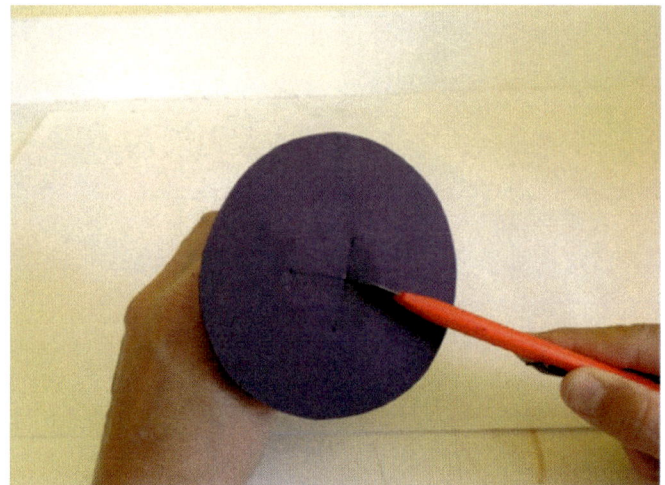

Using scissors or a utility knife, cut an 'x' in the bottom of the hat. Cut the slits as far as the edge of the cone.

Press the tabs inward and apply glue.

Position the hat on the Witch's head. The 'x' in the hat should allow it to slide right down onto the head when positioned correctly. Twist the hat around to allow this to happen. Press firmly in place until the glue sets.

Using the pattern piece for the nose, make a cone following the same directions that you used to make the hat. Trim to the desired length and/or to even up the edges.

Use the directions on **PAGE 17** for making the hair. Make it whatever color you like...blue, purple, black or even rainbow colored! Make about 8-10 clumps.

Put glue along the inside edge of the cone that you made for the nose.

Locate the upward pointing 'v' on the witch's face. This is where you will glue the nose.

Pinch the end of the cone onto the 'v' and hold in place until the glue sets.

Add the eyes and mouth. Use the patterns or be creative and make your own.

With children, it may be easier for them to make their hair out of strips of paper and let them glue it on with tacky glue, (see **PAGE 33**). When making them on your own, I recommend using a hot glue gun.

Glue the clumps of hair all around the head just below the rim of the hat. Place a small dab of glue on the back of the hat and press it to the hair to hold the rim down. This helps to cover the tops of the clumps of hair.

Here is the completed head of your Witch. Go ahead and add a wart on her nose or a spider on the rim of her hat.

With a red marker, make stripes on both sides of each leg piece.

Put a small amount of glue at the bottom of one of the legs. Glue it to the top of the boot as shown above.

Put some glue on the tabs that are at the bottom of the boot. Fold each tab in so they line up evenly with the bottom of the leg.

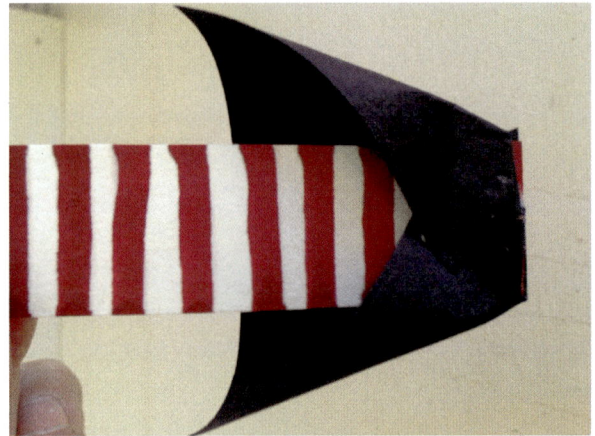

When both tabs are glued and folded in, the top of the Witch's boot is created.

Fold the sole of the Witch's boot where the heel meets the front. Put some glue around the bottom of the Witch's leg / boot and insert into the fold on the sole.

Once the glue has had a chance to set, unfold the sole of the boot and fold the back and front down, creating a heel on the bottom.

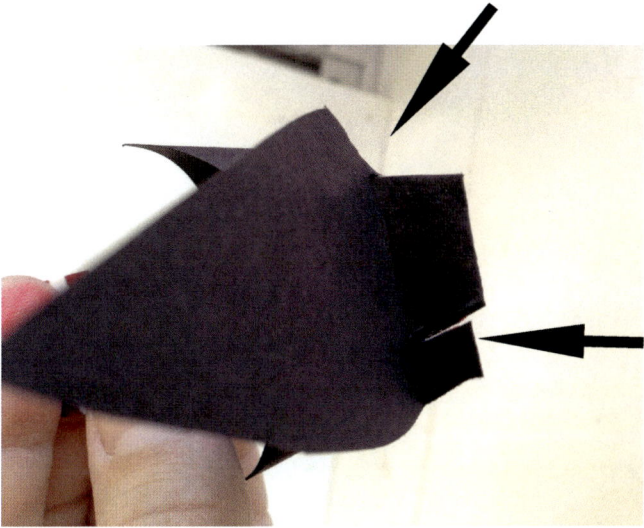

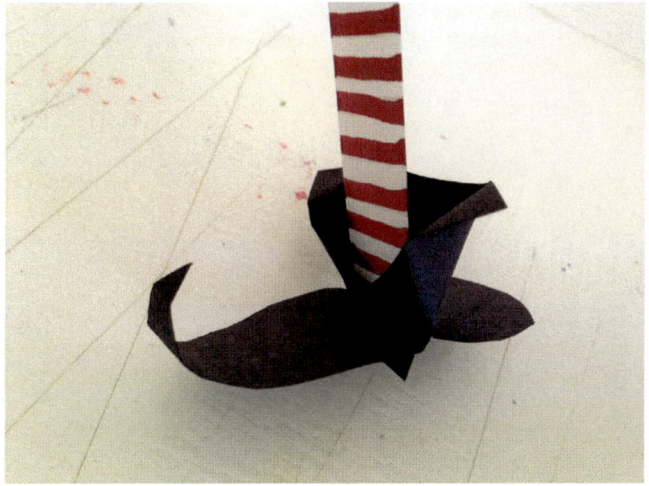

Snip the heel on both sides to the desired width and trim off the pieces. You will need to shape the sole of the boot once this is done by rounding up edges you just trimmed.

Finally, curl up the toes of the boots and fold down the corners of the boot tops to complete these dainty little booties.

Draw a line around the Witch's waist, beginning at the bottom of the 'v' on her front. Put glue on one of the lines on the front of her body. Place the first skirt piece on her waist starting at the 'v'.

Glue on the second skirt piece, overlapping the first just slightly. If you look at the Witch's body, there are four sections to go around with the skirt pieces. There should be two pieces glued in each section.

Continue all the way around the waist with two skirt pieces in each section, using the line that you drew as a guide.

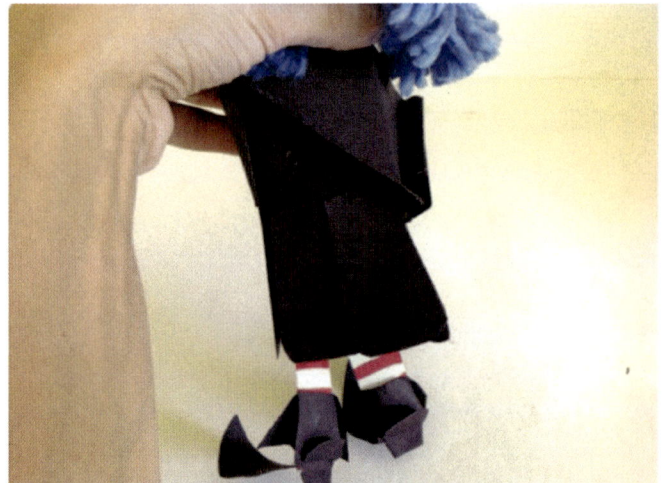

Eight skirt pieces should bring you all around the Witch's body.

Trim about 1/2" off the top of the last four skirt pieces. These will be used to "puff" the skirt.

At the front seam where the two sections of the skirt come together, apply glue along the underside edges.

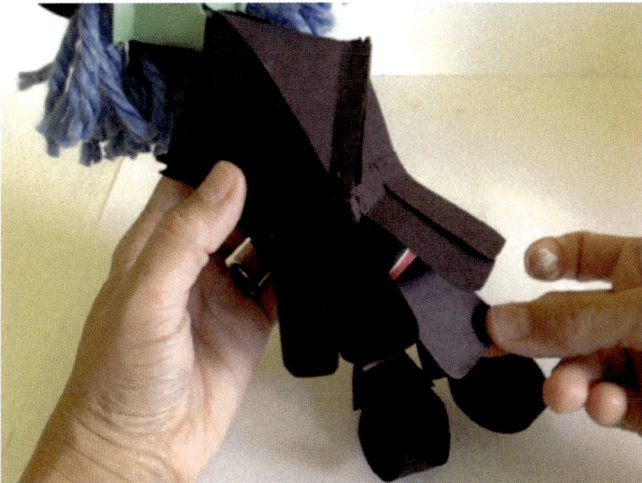

Slide one of the trimmed skirt pieces up under the skirt and push it up to the waist. Spread the two skirt pieces apart as you stick this piece to the glue you just applied.

As you can see, this added piece allows the skirt to "puff" out rather than lay flat. The more you spread these pieces apart as you glue, the more the skirt will stick out.

Do the same with the other three skirt pieces to allow the skirt to puff out.
Go back around and glue each skirt piece to its neighbor.

Use a piece of ribbon or paper to glue around the Witch's waist as a belt. This will also cover up the top parts of the skirt pieces.

What a cute little lady! Here is her skirt and belt all finished!

Use the directions on **PAGE 16** to make and attach the arms.

Make the arm cuff using the trapezoid pattern piece. Put glue along one of the side edges and wrap around the arm. The long edge of the trapezoid goes toward the hand and the pointed part of the cuff points down.

Cut out the two collar pieces for the Witch's dress. Apply glue along the short edge.

Lift her hair slightly and attach the collar to her back/shoulder. Attach the other in the same way. You can decide how high you want the collar to stick up, or if you even want to have a collar at all.

Your witch is now complete!

Add buttons to the front of her dress for some added decoration and try various ways to give her different personalities. Change the colors of her skin, her dress or the stripes of her stockings. Make her hair out of different materials or in different colors. Give her big google eyes instead of paper eyes. There are endless possibilities to make the Witch into a new and exciting character each time she is made.

Have fun!!

The Turkey

TURKEY

MATERIALS

	Color	Paper
Body (2 chompers)	Dark brown	6" X 9"
Head (2 chompers)	Dark Brown	4 1/2" X 6"
Beak (x1), Feet (x1)	Orange	Use patterns
Hat / Neck Pieces (x1 each)	Black / White	Use pattern
Eyes (x2)	Outside white / inside black	Use pattern
Wings (x2)	Tan	Use patterns
Tail Feathers	Orange, Green, Yellow	9" x 12" (orange), 8" x 12" (green), 7" x 12" (yellow)
Wattle	Red	Use pattern
Other Materials	Tacky Glue, scissors, black permanent marker	Heavy cardboard for base; yellow paper for hat buckle

GETTING STARTED

Begin by getting all of your pieces traced, cut and folded. Use the directions for 'The Chomper' on **PAGES 9-15** to make the head and body parts.

Pattern pieces for the rest of your character are included in the back of the book on **PAGES 115-118.**

The Turkey can be made to sit on a table as a centerpiece or you can leave off the heavy cardboard on the feet and hang him up instead.

Before I started making the Turkey out of Chompers with students, I would make them each year using paper lunch bags. All of the pattern pieces that are used for this version are the same, so go ahead and try the paper bag version if you'd like. It works very well with young children.

To begin, lightly crumple 1-2 pieces of newspaper and put it into the bottom of the lunch bag. Pinch the lunch bag about halfway up with the newspaper filling up the Turkey's tummy. Where you pinch the bag becomes the neck. Tie a piece of string tightly around the neck (or use scotch tape).

Spread out the remaining opening of the bag. Tightly crumple about a half sheet of newspaper into a ball and place it into the top of the paper bag. This is the Turkey's head. Fold the top of the bag over the newspaper and tape closed. You now have the Turkey's head and body.

Add the remaining pieces following the given directions.

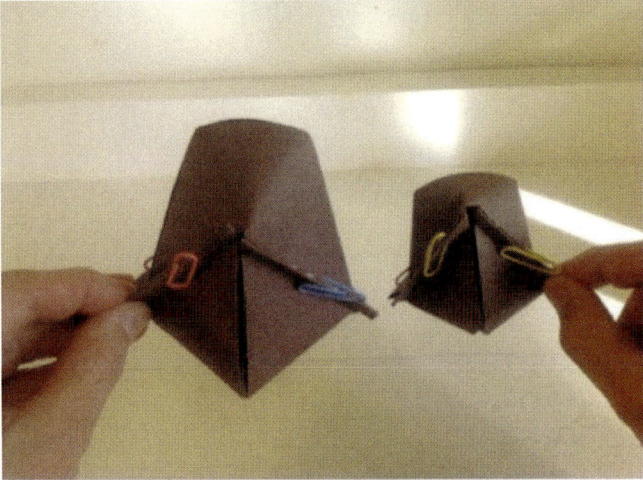

Make the head and body using the directions on **PAGES 9-14.**

Attach the head to the body using the directions on **PAGE 15**.

Insert two orange tabs into the bottom of the turkey in the same way that you did to attach the head.

Cover the piece of cardboard with a thin layer of glue, getting out to all of the edges.

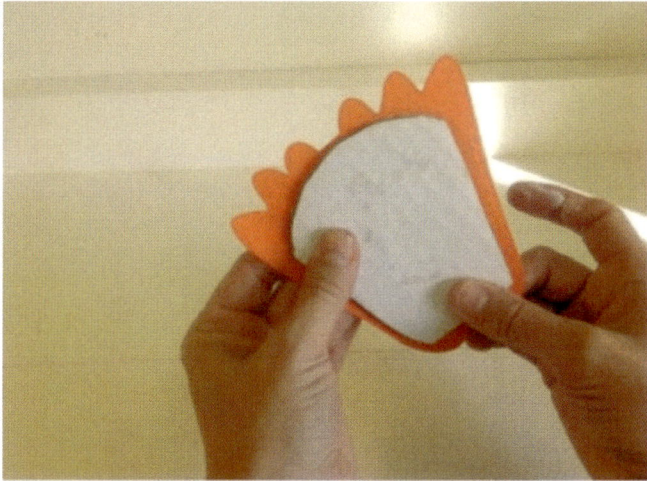

Glue the piece of cardboard to the Turkey's feet.

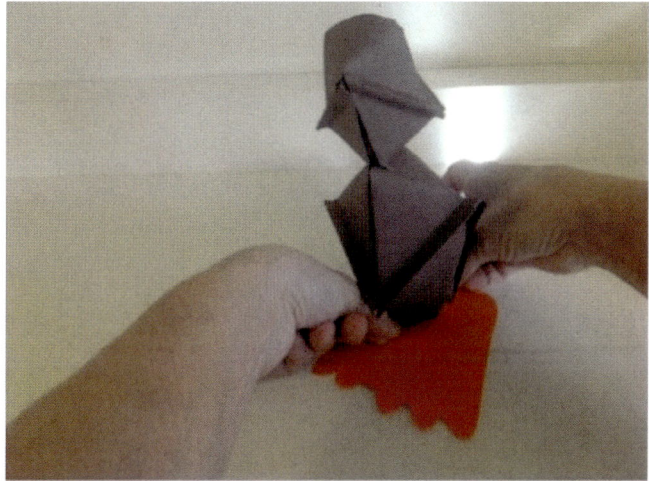

Attach the Turkey's body to his feet in the same way that you attached the head to the body. Be sure to position the body as you like before gluing down. The more you pull the tabs apart as you glue the less wobbly he'll be.

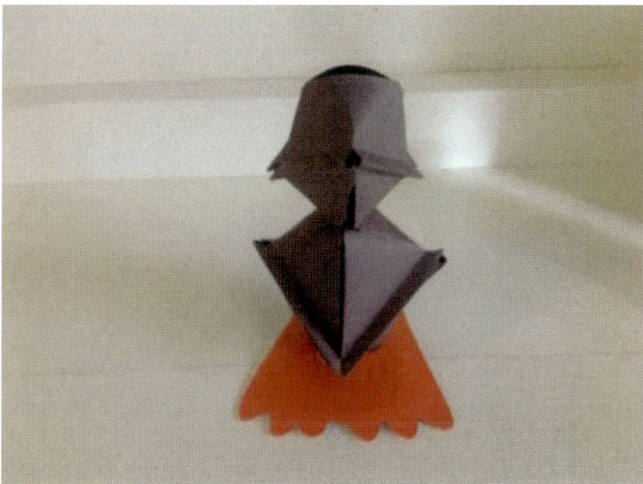

This is the Turkey's body with the feet attached. The cardboard allows him to stand alone so he can be used as a centerpiece for your Thanksgiving table.

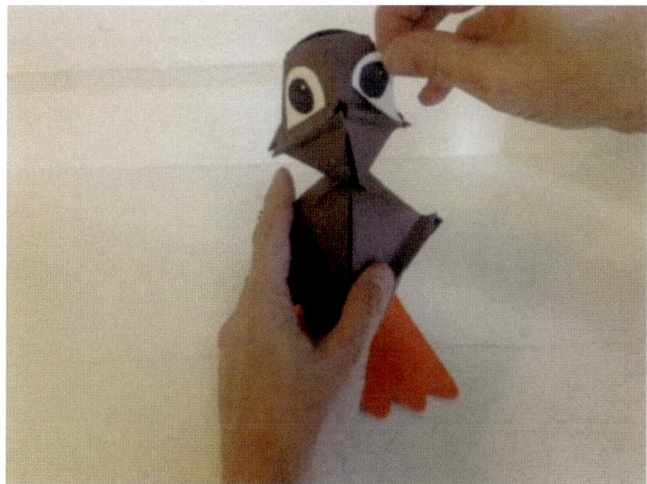

Cut out and attach the eyes as shown.

Apply glue along half of the straight edge of the beak.

Curl the sides toward each other to create a cone and hold until the glue sets.
Trim the beak to the desired size.

Put glue along the inside edge of the cone.

Place the cone over the 'v' on the Turkey's face and pinch until it stays in place.

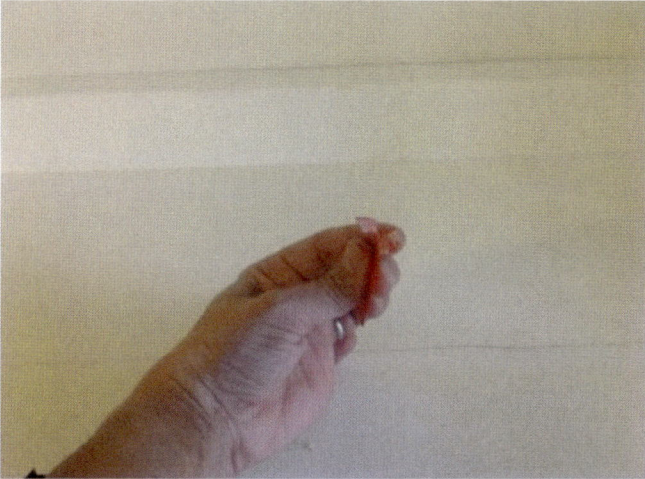

Cut a slit in the flat edge of the red *wattle*.
Fold one tab forward and the other tab back.
Apply glue to both tabs.

Glue the wattle to the underside of the
Turkey's beak. Some people like to glue the
wattle hanging down from the top of the beak
rather than the bottom.

He's coming along nicely. Now you need his hat and collar piece.

Glue the black collar piece to the white.

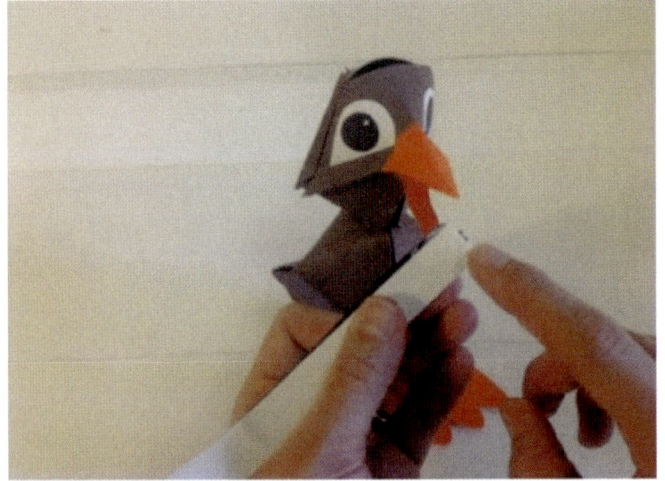

Put some glue on the edge of the collar and wrap it around his neck.

When gluing, be sure that the white part of the collar is centered just below the beak.

For the hat, glue the white strip onto the black rectangle about 1/2" from the bottom.

Fold the edge of the rectangle in about 1/2"to where the white strip begins.. Make snips along the edge, about 1/2" apart and going in as far as the fold that you made.

Fold the other long edge in about 1/2" and make snips along the length in the same way.

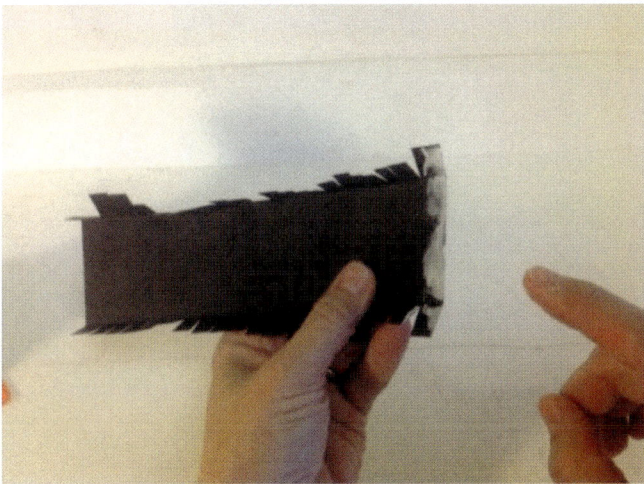

Put some glue on the inside of one of the short edges.

Wrap the rectangle around to form a tube, holding in place until the glue sets. Try to make the white strip line up when you glue.

Fold all of the tabs of the tube inward. Apply glue to the tabs on one end, making sure to get glue right out to the edges.

Cut out the square piece for the hat and center it onto the tube that you just made.

Hold/press the square firmly to the tube and the tabs until it is secure. You may want to put your finger into the hat and press the tabs down from the inside.

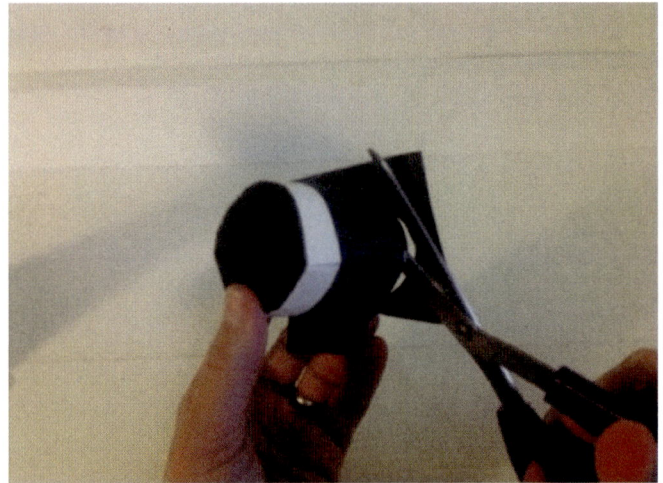

Be sure that the glue is fairly dry before using your scissors to trim away the extra. It helps to view the hat from below as you trim so you can see the tube as you cut.

Cut out the circle for the hat and center it onto the tube that you just made.

Using scissors or a utility knife, cut an 'x' in the bottom of the hat. Cut out as far as the edge of the tube.

Push the tabs in a bit and apply glue, making sure to get right to the edges.

Position the hat on the Turkey's head. The 'x' in the hat should allow it to slide right down onto the head when positioned correctly. Twist the hat around to allow this to happen.

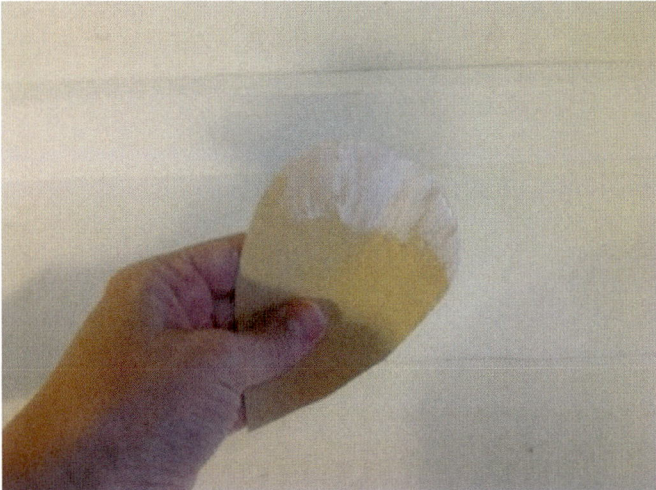

Add glue to the rounded part of the wings.

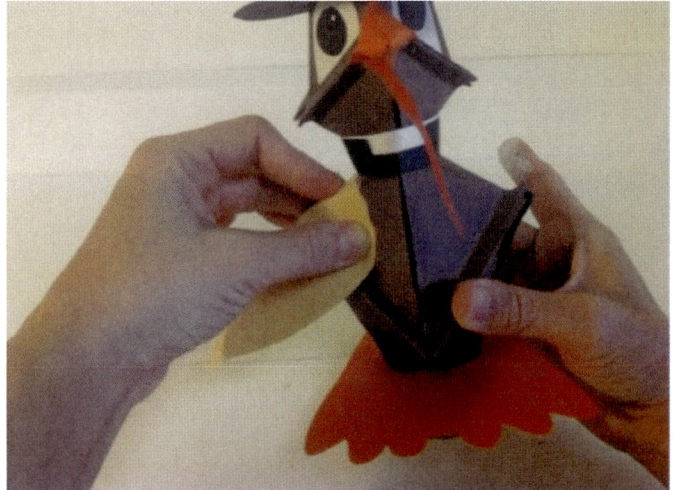

Wrap the wing over the shoulder and hold in place until the glue sets.

He's looking good! Time for the tail!

Cut the tail pieces to the indicated sizes and lay them on top of each other as shown above.

See **PAGE 62** for an easier/alternate tail.

Make the first fold about 1" wide and continue to make an accordion fold with all three pieces of paper together.

Fold the paper in half centering it the best that you can. The paper is thick and can be a little tricky to manage at times.

Keeping the paper folded like a fan, use a piece of masking or duct tape to wrap around the base to hold in place.

Find the center seam where the pieces come together and add some glue.

Pinch the center where you put glue to connect the center of the tail. Hold until the glue sets.

Pull the tail open as far it will go. To keep the tail open, attach a piece of tape to the last fold on the bottom of the tail, wrap over the base that you have already taped and attach to the last fold on the other side of the tail.

From the front, your tail will look like this.

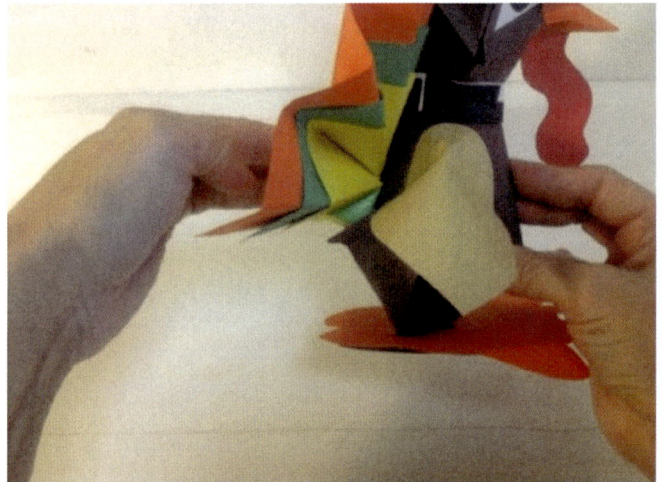

The best way to glue on the tail is with a hot glue gun. When making this with children, I glue the tail on for them. Put a fair amount of glue onto the base where you taped and press to the Turkey's back just above the 'v'.

Here he is, all ready to dress up your Thanksgiving table.

Try changing colors around or sticking a feather in his head rather than putting on a hat. For the tail, trace hands in different colors, write what you are thankful for and glue them on as his feathers rather than doing the accordion fold.

As with all of these characters, make him your own and begin some new family traditions by bringing him out each year to celebrate.

Using your choice of colors for the tail feathers, cut out the circle and about 8-10 feathers in each color. Trim one of the sets of feathers to be a bit smaller than the other color.

Put glue along the edge of the circle about 3/4 of the way around. Start at one end with the shorter set of feathers and glue them on, overlapping slightly as you work your way around to the other side.

Turn the tail completely over. Again, put glue along the edge on this side of the circle about 3/4 of the way around.

Start at one side with the longer feathers and glue them on, overlapping slightly. Place these feathers so they fall BETWEEN the shorter feathers. When finished, glue to the back of the Turkey with Tacky Glue.

Santa

SANTA

MATERIALS

	Color	Paper
Body (2 chompers)	Red	6" X 9"
Head (2 chompers)	Flesh / Tan	4 1/2" X 6"
Mouth	Pink	Use patterns
Beard / Mustache (x1 each)	White	Use pattern
Eyes (x2)	Outside white / inside black	Use pattern
Jacket Bottom (x11), Arms (x2), Legs (x2), Hat (x1)	Red	Use patterns
Boots (x2 each piece)	Black	Use patterns
Mittens (x2)	Green	Use pattern
Other Materials	Tacky Glue, scissors, buttons, small glasses/wire (optional)	cotton, white yarn, yellow paper for belt buckle, pink pompom

GETTING STARTED

Begin by getting all of your pieces
traced, cut and folded. Use the
directions for 'The Chomper' on
PAGES 9-15
to make the head and body parts.

Pattern pieces for the rest of your
character are included in the back
of the book on **PAGES 119-121**

As with The Witch, the Santa has never been made with children and is probably
the most involved character in this book. Again, simply adapt whatever seems
tricky in order to make it work for kids. Oftentimes, they will just do it their own
way and come up with something new and imaginative that has never been done
before. Try giving them the pieces and see what they do with them.

With children, I would recommend using the simple directions for attaching the
arms and legs on **PAGES 16-17** and use cotton for the hair. Rather than making
boots, children can put fur at the bottom of the pant leg just as they did with the
sleeve. You can even eliminate the bottom of the jacket and just put a belt around
Santa's waist.

No matter how you decide to use the directions and pattern pieces to make your
own, unique Santa, you will discover that the final creation is simply amazing. You
will be awed by what your children do and by what you are able to create on your
own with just paper, scissors, glue and some easy to find craft supplies.

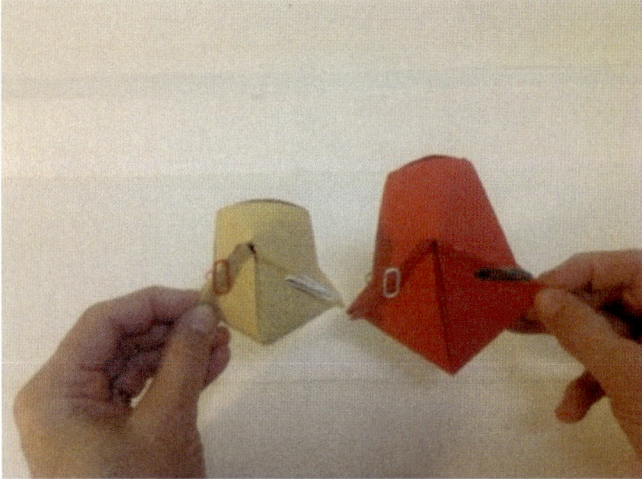

Using the directions on **PAGES 9-14**, make a tan head and a red body for your Santa.

Attach the head to the body using the directions on **PAGES 15-16.** Glue on the eyes. I decided to give my Santa blue eyes.

Glue on the pink mouth piece just below the nose.

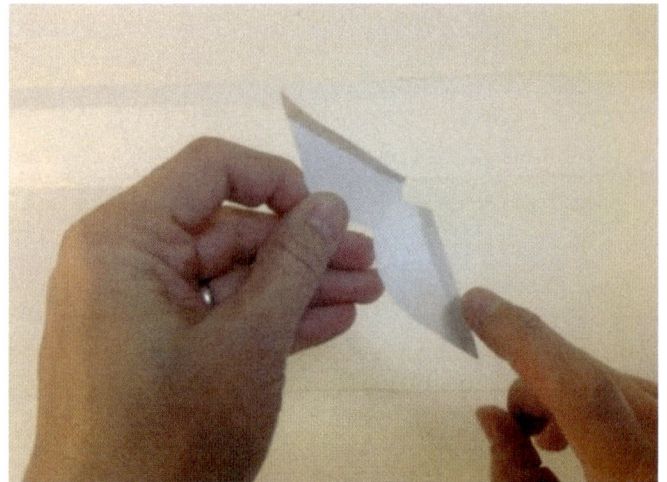

Fold down the flat edges of the mustache about 1/4". Apply glue to the inside fold.

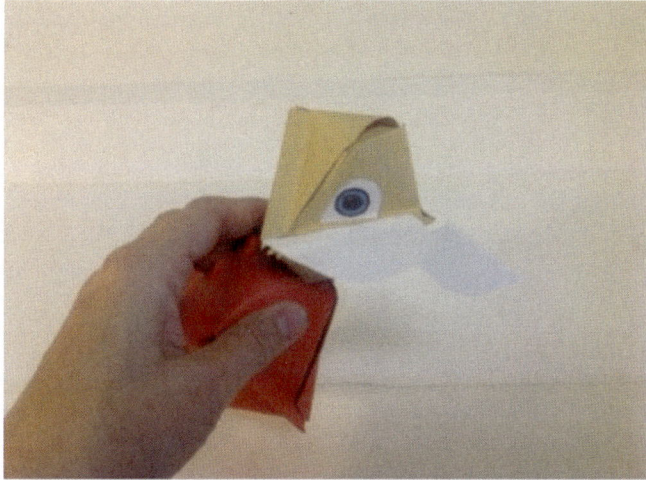

Glue the mustache to the 'v' shaped rim on Santa's face. Make the 'v' *notch* in the top of the mustache line up with the tip of the nose.

Wrap the mustache around to the other side of the face and glue down.

Snip off the tip of Santa's nose (the tan point) in order to have a flat spot to glue on the pompom nose.

Here is your Santa waiting for his beard and nose.

Apply glue around Santa's neck to glue on his fur collar, which is made out of a cotton ball.

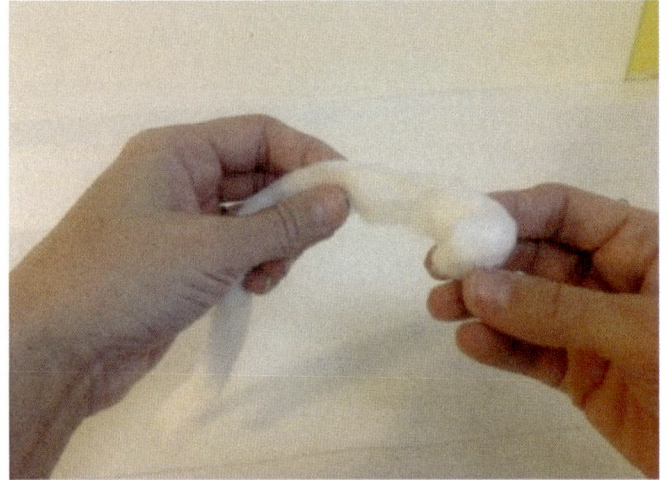

Some cotton balls can actually be unrolled, which works perfectly for projects like this. I used Jumbo cotton balls and simply unrolled them into a long strand of cotton.

If your cotton balls do not unroll, stretch them out and roll them between your palms to create a long, snake-like strand of cotton. Wrap the cotton around Santa's neck where you applied the glue.

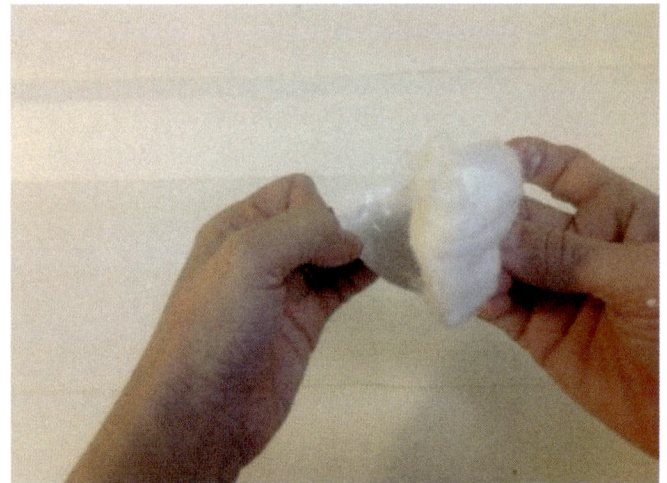

Cut the white beard out of paper. Spread glue over the entire piece and stick on some cotton. You may wish to pull the cotton ball apart a bit to make his beard more fluffy.

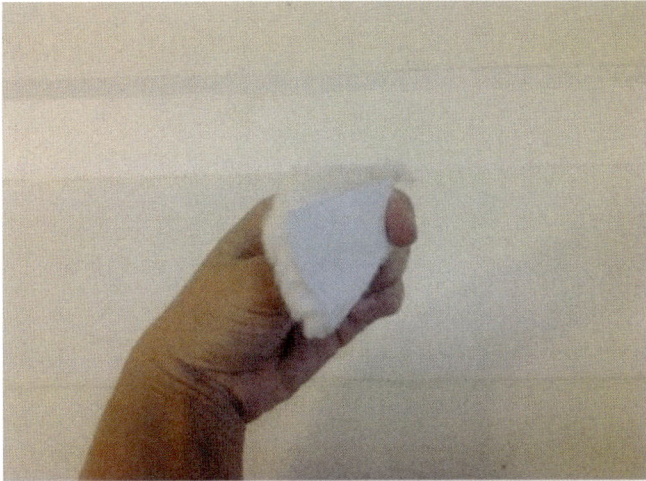

Once you have covered the beard with cotton, one side should be just be paper. This is the side that will get glued to Santa's face.

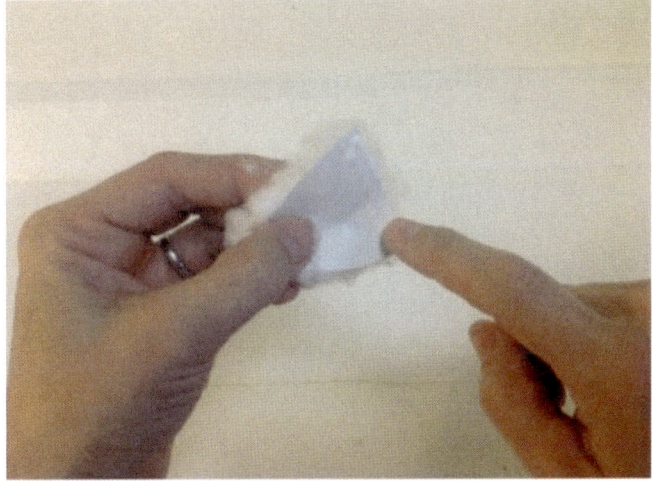

Cover the paper on the beard with glue. Be sure to get to the edges and try to keep the glue away from the cotton. It gets messy very quickly if you get a gluey finger into the cotton.

Glue the beard onto Santa's face just below his mustache. Be sure that you can still see the pink part of his mouth through the beard.

Pull a cotton ball apart to make it lighter and fluffier to make it easier to glue on for the mustache.

Cover the paper mustache with glue.

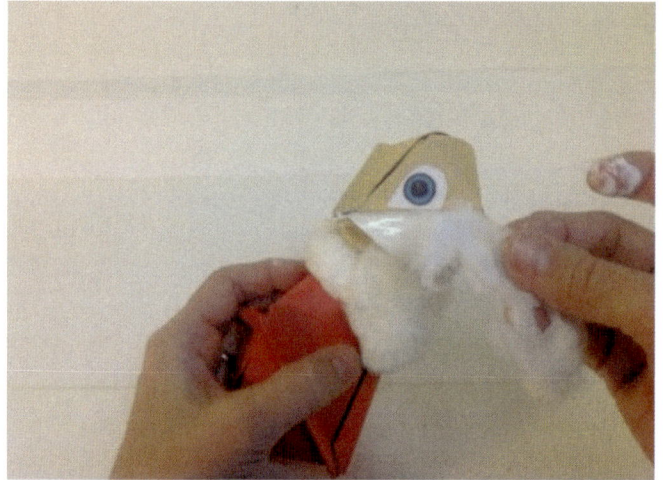

Carefully stick the fluffy cotton onto the mustache, covering the paper as much as possible.

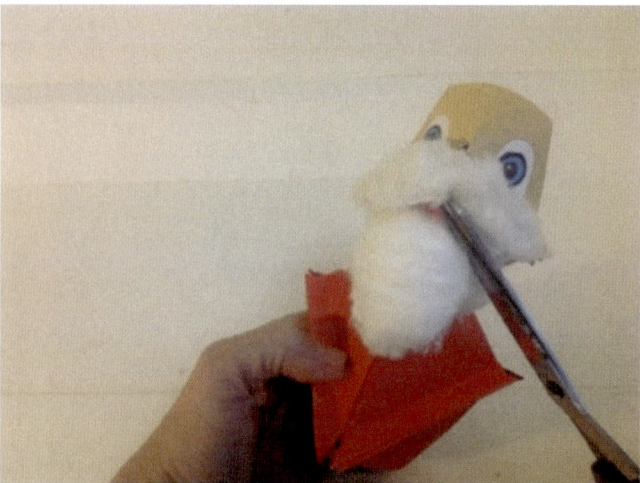

Once the beard and mustache are all glued on and in place, give Santa a little trim to cut away any loose pieces of cotton. Trim along the mustache, especially the bottom part, in order to maintain the shape.

Using tacky glue or a hot glue gun, glue Santa's nose on. It should cover the hole that you created when you snipped his 'nose'.

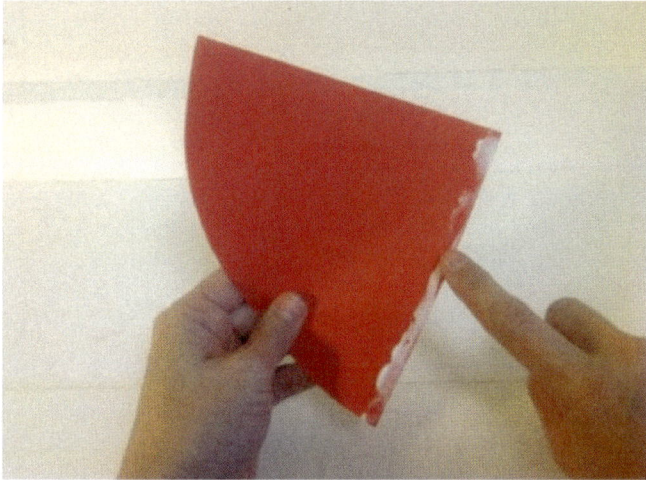

Apply glue along one flat edge of Santa's hat.

Roll the paper to form a cone and glue the edge down. Hold until the glue sets.

Put glue along the inside edge of Santa's hat.

Place the hat on Santa's head, leaning it toward the back so it does not cover his eyes and so it rests over the point on the back of his head.

Pinch the front and the back of the hat to Santa's head and hold until the glue sets.

Pinch his hat together about halfway up.

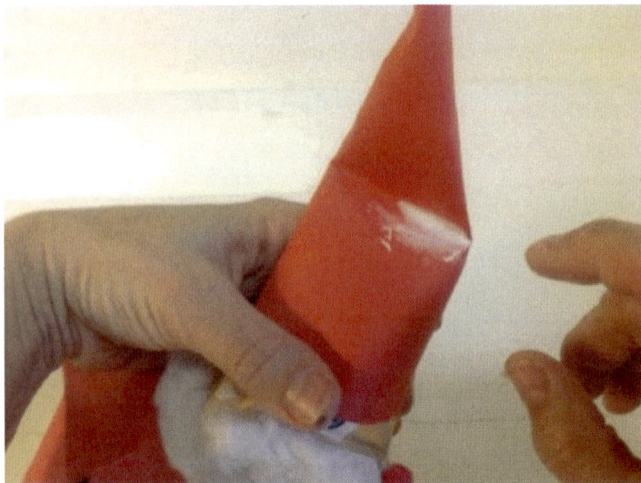

Put a little bit of glue into the fold.

Bend the hat in half and hold with a paper clip until dry.

MAKING AND ATTACHING THE HAIR

Using the directions on **PAGES 17-18**, make 8-10 clumps of hair for Santa's head.

If making these with children, use cotton for his hair and attach with tacky glue or make hair out of paper (see **PAGE 33**). When I make them on my own, I use yarn and glue the hair on with a hot glue gun.

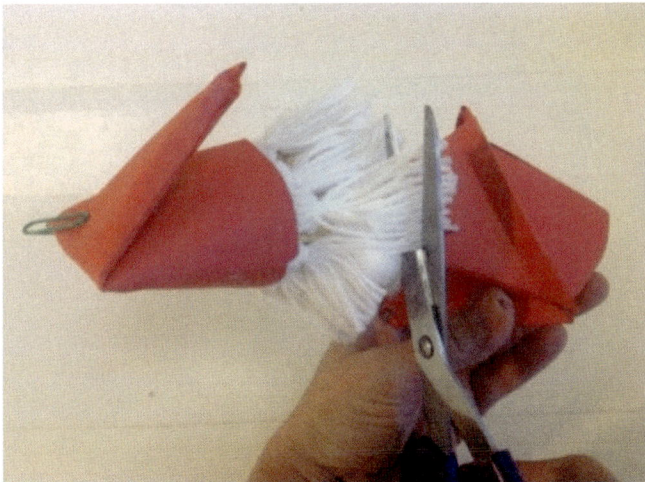

Once you have glued the clumps of hair all around Santa's head, just at the base of the hat, trim his hair to the desired length.

Glue a strand of cotton around the base of the hat to cover the top of the hair and to make the fur on Santa's hat.

MAKING AND ATTACHING THE POMPOM

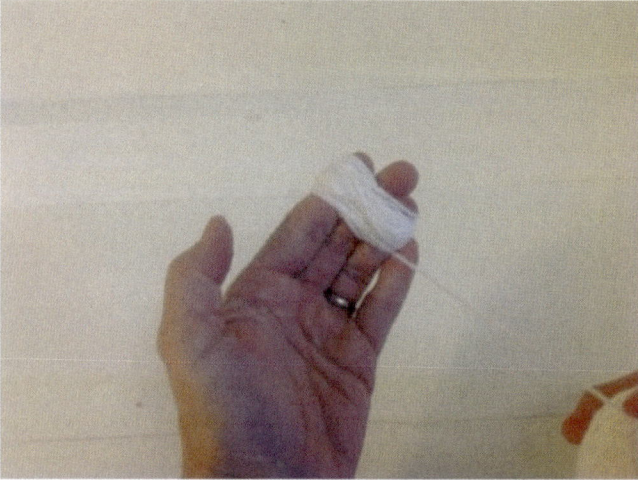

To make the pompom for Santa's hat, wrap white yarn around your fingers 20-30 times.

To make it easier, use store purchased pompoms and glue onto the tip of the hat.

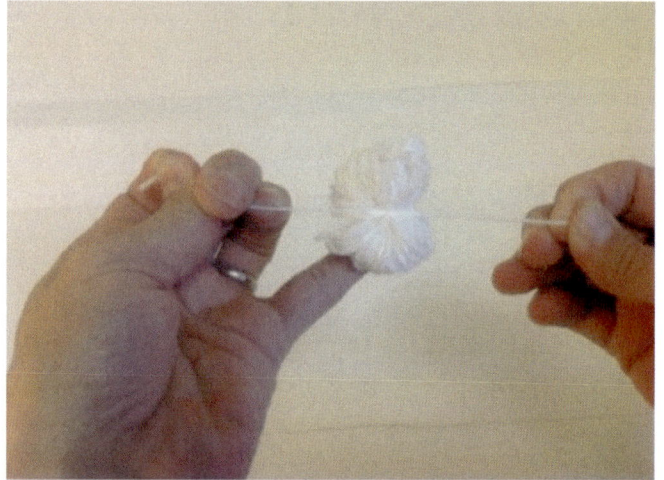

Slide the loops of yarn off of your fingers. Using a piece of string (about 6" long), tie a tight, double knot around the center of the loops.

Place your scissors through the loops on both ends and snip the loops. Move the pieces of string around and snip through any loops that you missed.

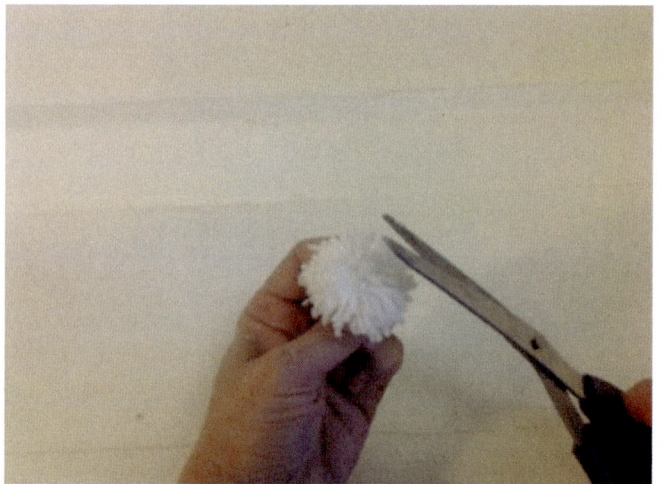

Fluff up the pompom and trim to make it more even and rounded. You should still have the two strings that you tied the loops with dangling down.

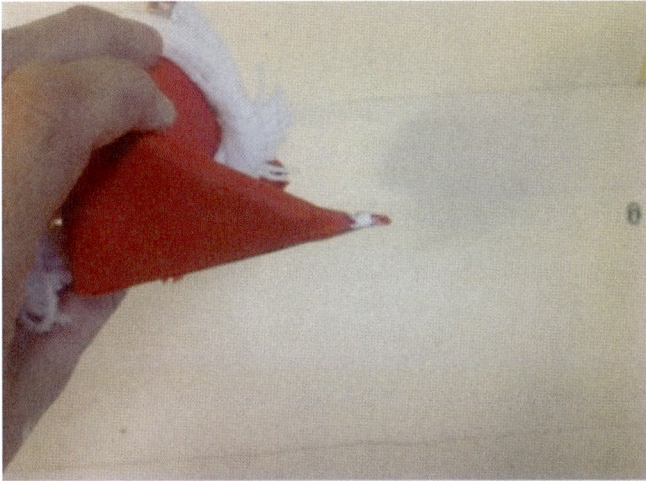

Pinch the end of Santa's hat and apply a small bit of glue to hold the string in place for the pompom.

Using the two strings on the pompom, tightly tie a double knot, attaching the pompom to the tip of the hat. Be sure to tie the knot so it touches the glue. This will keep the pompom from sliding off.

What a handsome man. Santa's head is complete and he's ready for some arms and legs.

MAKING AND ATTACHING THE ARMS

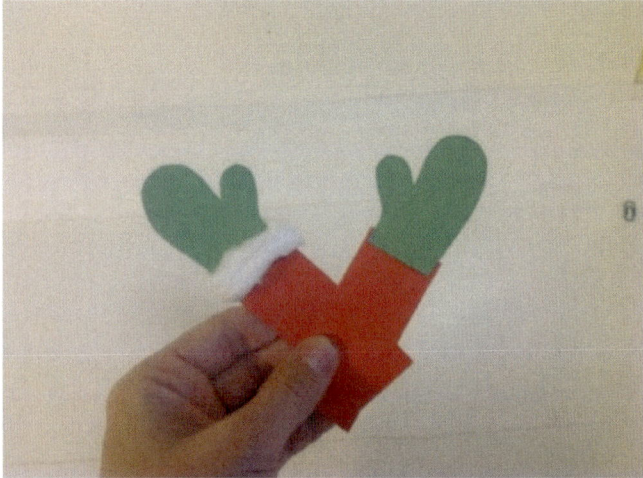

Use the directions on **PAGE 16** for making the arms. Glue and wrap some cotton around the wrist for the fur cuff.

Attach the arms using the directions on **PAGE 16.** Bend at the elbow.

His arms are now complete and it's time to make the legs.

Glue the small black squares to the bottom of the red leg strips. These are to make black tabs to attach the legs to the boots.

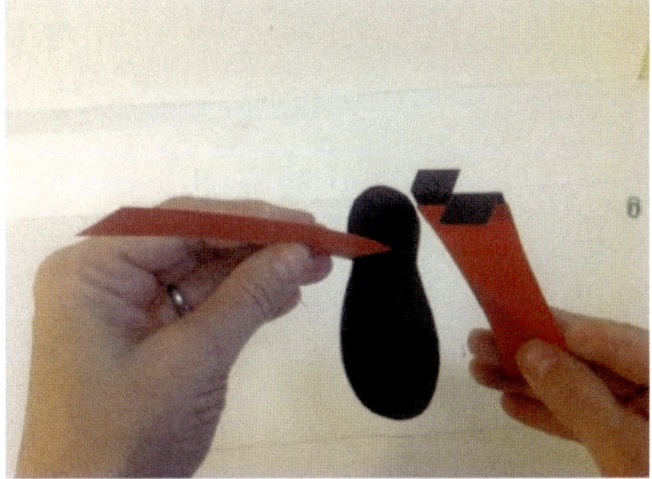

Use the directions on **PAGE 17** for attaching the shoes to the legs. Be sure to make the tabs from the black paper.

Glue a strip of cotton across the long end of the trapezoid for the fur at the top of Santa's boot. Put some glue along the inside edge of the trapezoids and wrap around Santa's leg (see Scarecrow directions on **PAGE 29**).

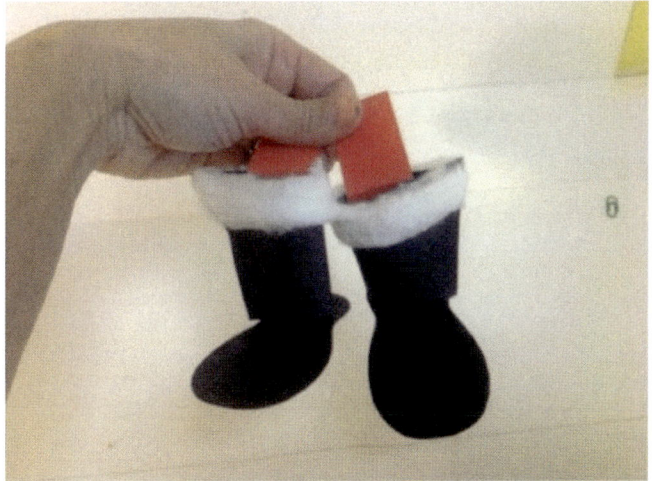

The cotton goes at the top and the pointed part of the boot cuff points to the outside. Bend the legs at the knee. Use the directions on **PAGE 17** to attach the legs to the body.

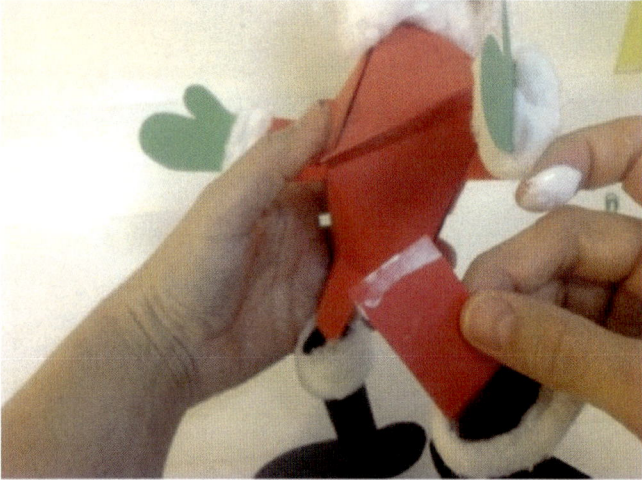

Put some glue along the top edge of one of the jacket pieces. Line it up with the downward pointing 'v' on Santa's front and glue it on. This is your guide to go all the way around the waist...draw a line lightly with pencil if it helps.

Glue the second jacket piece overlapping the first just slightly. If you look at Santa's body, there are four sections to go around with the jacket pieces. There should be two pieces glued into each section.

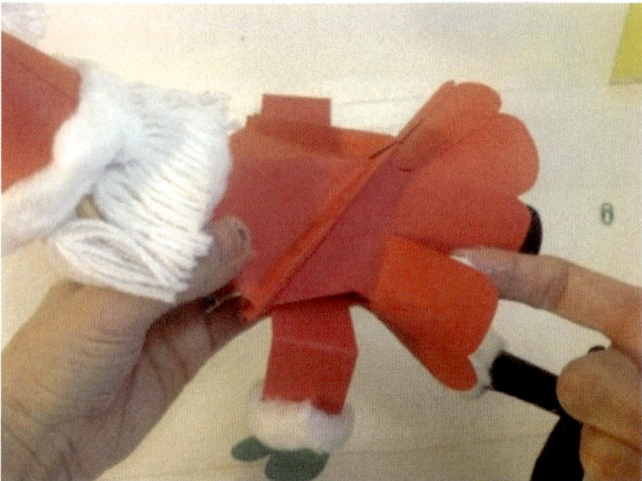

Continue all the way around the waist with two skirt pieces in each section. Eight jacket pieces should bring you all around Santa's body.

Use the directions on **PAGE 42** to complete the bottom of Santa's jacket. DO NOT glue a jacket piece across the front seam of the jacket. Leave that open. Go back around the jacket glueing each piece to its neighbor.

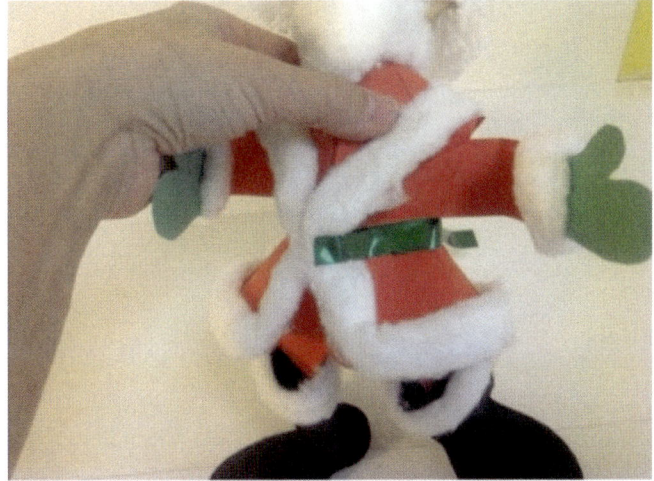

Starting at Santa's shoulder, run glue along the 'v' on his chest, down along one side and along the bottom of his jacket. Attach a strip of cotton or thick cotton yarn to the jacket for the fur. Do this on both sides of the jacket until the cotton meets in the back.

Using a piece of ribbon or foil paper, wrap and glue Santa's belt tightly around his waist.

Cut out a golden buckle and glue to the front of his belt. Attach two buttons on the front of his jacket as well.

If you desire, you can make Santa a pair of glasses out of pipe cleaners or craft wire. You can often find small pairs of glasses for dolls in craft stores or online if you choose to purchase them.

Your Santa is complete. Make him a sack to carry all of his toys using a brown paper lunch bag. Wrap a small gift for him to carry in his hands. Try different colored eyes, mittens or belt.

Welcome your Santa into your home this holiday season and for many years to come.

The Snowman

THE SNOWMAN

MATERIALS

	Color	Paper
Head (2 chompers)	White	6" X 9"
Middle (2 choppers)	White	4 1/2" X 6"
Bottom (2 chompers)	White	9" X 9"
Hat (1 each piece)	Black	Use pattern
Eyes (x2)	Black	buttons
Scarf	Your choice of fabric	2" x 18"
Arms	-	2 sticks, about 6" long each
Nose	Orange	Use pattern
Other Materials	Tacky Glue, scissors, buttons, ribbon or foil paper for hat	If sticks are unavailable, make out of heavy paper/cardboard and attach

GETTING STARTED

Begin by getting all of your pieces traced, cut and folded. Use the directions for 'The Chomper' on **PAGES 9-15** to make the head and body parts.

Pattern pieces for the rest of your character are included in the back of the book on **PAGES 122-123.**

Mr. Snowman has graced the ceilings of my classrooms for many, many years. He has been a tradition that families look forward to making each year when their children come into my room.   Living in the Northeast Kingdom of Vermont, children have a lot of experience in making real snowmen. If you live in a place where that is just not possible, now you can begin your own traditions of making snowmen with your children and students.

If you have REALLY BIG PAPER, like poster board size, you can increase the pattern sizes and make a REALLY BIG SNOWMAN! I have done this before with different characters and the result is simply amazing. Picture a row of three foot snowmen, all decked out in their fancy top hats and scarves, lined up in the hallway ready to greet parents for a holiday event. It will be the talk of the town.

One year, instead of top hats, we put fleece beanies and felt mittens on our snowmen. There are many great books out there to read and attach a writing project to go along. Have your snowmen hold onto paper shovels that serve as the 'frame' for their piece of writing.

Using the directions on **PAGES 9-14** make the head and the bottom of the snowman.

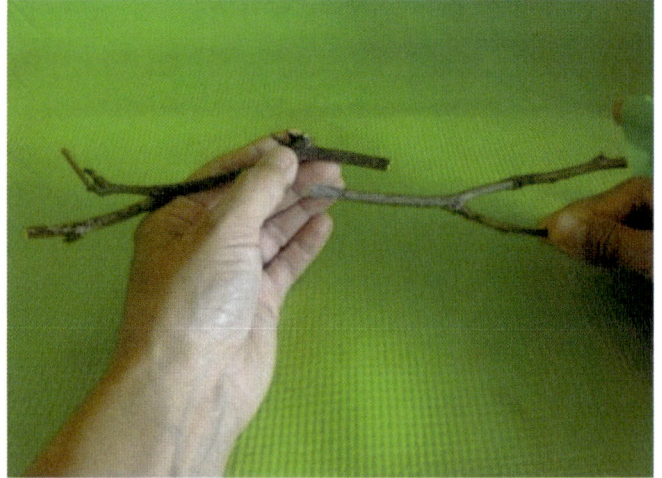

Place your two sticks end-to-end with a slight overlap and the 'fingers' pointing outward. Your sticks should be about 6" in length and have extra branches for fingers.

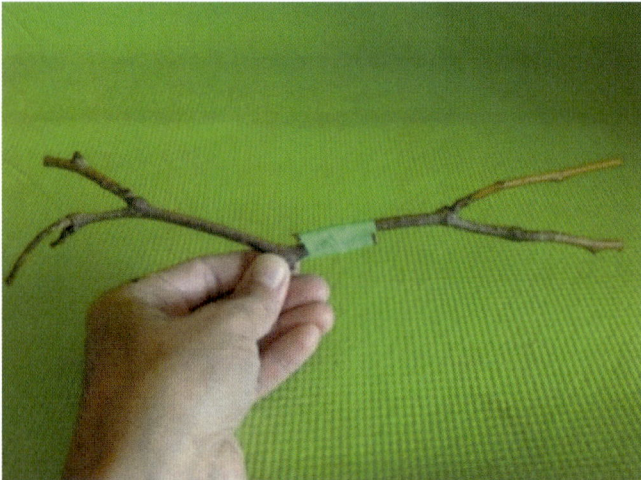

Wrap tape around the sticks to hold them together.

Apply glue around the four lips of the Chomper for the middle part of the body.

Lay the sticks in the mouth of the Chomper so the tape is centered.

This may be tricky to do alone so extra hands may be helpful. Attach the Chompers as you did for the head and bottom, keeping the sticks in the middle as you glue.

When the middle part is together, the two stick arms will poke out the sides.

Use the directions on **PAGES 15-16** to attach the head to the middle section.

Now that the head is attached, it is time to attach the bottom.

Begin by gluing in the tabs onto the bottom of the middle section as described on **PAGE 15**.

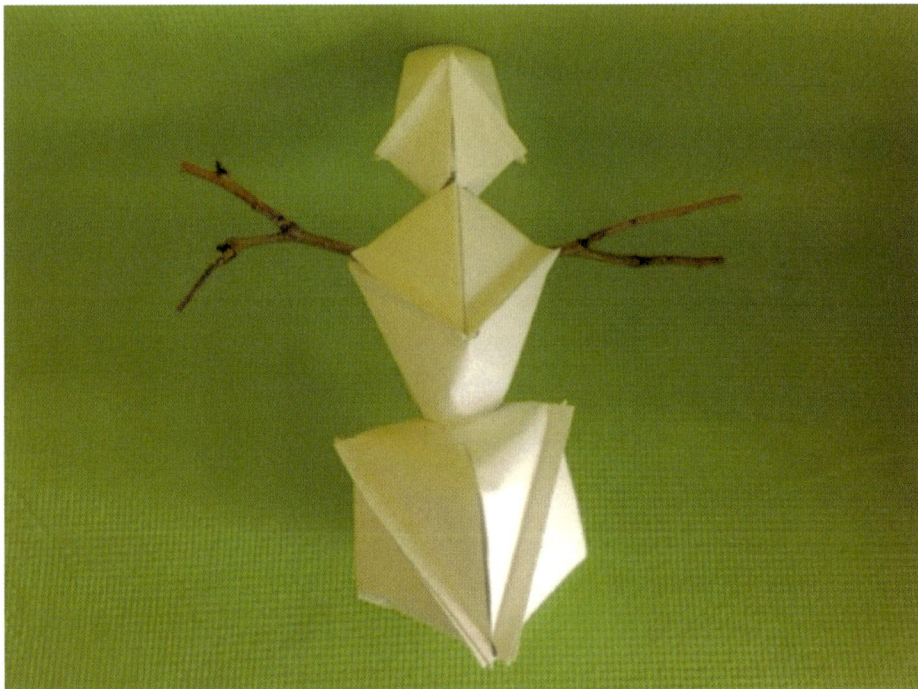

Using the directions on **PAGE 16** attach the middle section to the bottom.

Apply glue along half of the straight edge of the nose piece.

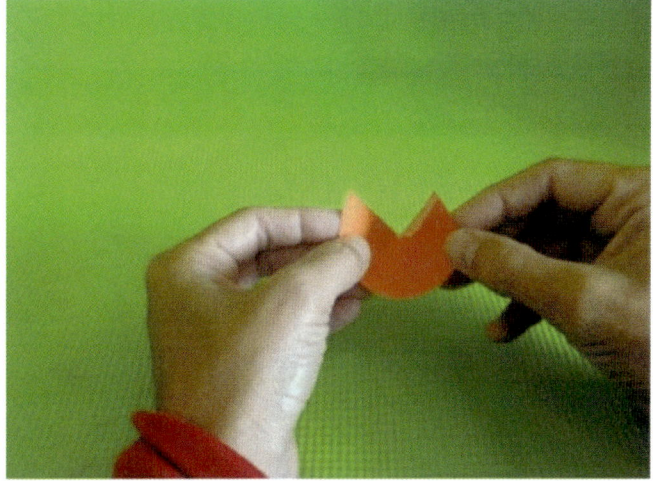

Bend the corner of the nose toward the center and wrap the glued edge around to create a cone.

Overlap the edges of the cone and hold in place until the glue sets. Overlap as much as you wish to create a wider or thinner nose.

The nose cone is complete. Trim to the desired length and/or to even up the edges.

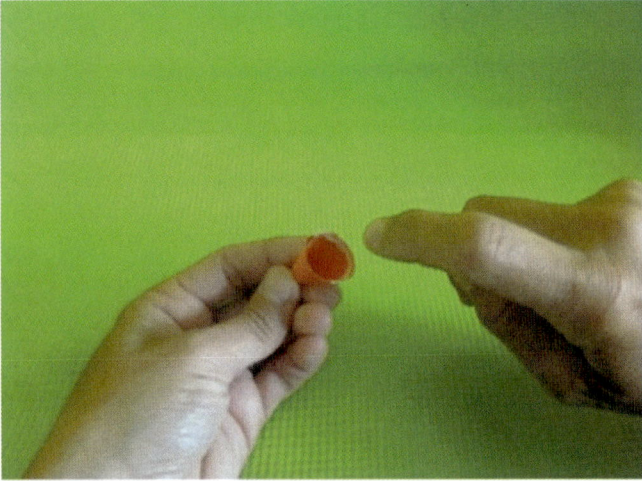

Put glue around the inside edge of the cone.

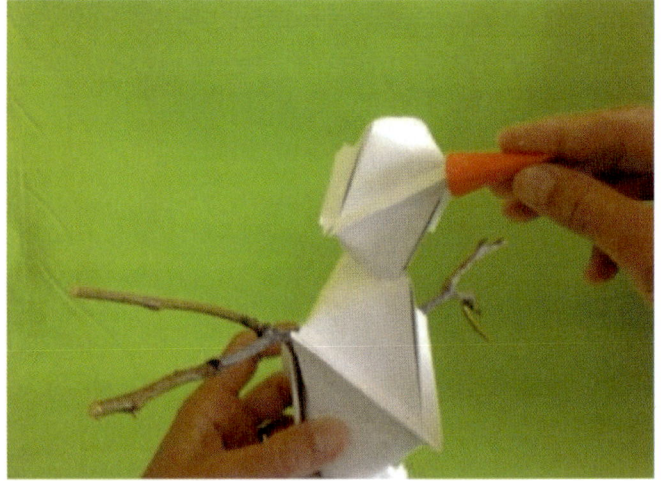

Place the cone on the upward pointing 'v' on the Snowman's face.

Pinch the Snowman's nose onto the face until it stays in place.

When glued on, the opening of the nose takes on the shape of the Snowman's face.

Fold each long edge of the rectangle inward about 1/2".

Snip along the folded edges. Snips should be about 1/2" apart and go as deep as the fold.

Put glue on the inside edge of one of the short sides of the rectangle.

Curl the rectangle around to form a tube and hold until the glue sets.

Push the tabs inward and cover them with glue, making sure to get to the edges.

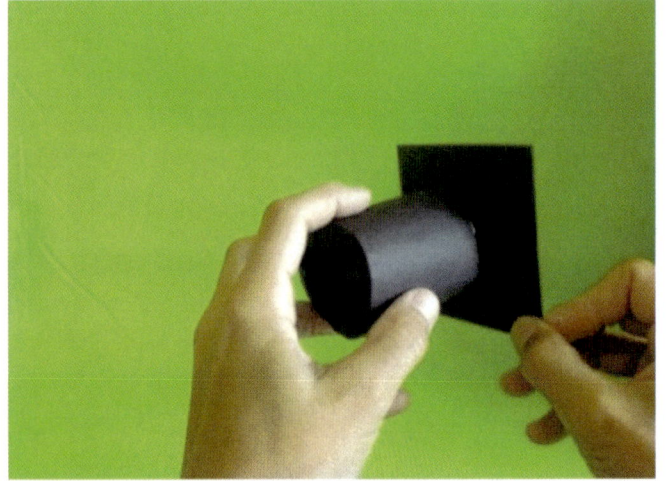

Firmly press the glued tabs onto the square piece of the hat.

Hold together until the pieces stay.

If needed, press the tabs down from the inside to get a secure hold.

When the glue is somewhat dry, trim the square piece away around the tube. It is easier to see where you are trimming if you hold the hat as shown.

This is the top of the hat.

Cover the tabs on the bottom of the hat with glue, making sure to get out the edges.

Center and firmly press the round part of the hat onto the tabs. Hold in place until the glue sets.

Using scissors or an utility knife cut an 'x' in the bottom of the hat. Cut outward as far as the edge of the tube.

The hat is almost ready to place on the Snowman. It needs a bit of color though.

Glue a strip of ribbon or paper around the base of the hat. Wrapping paper often makes nice hat strips.

Now your hat is ready for your Snowman!

Push the tabs inward a bit and cover them with glue, making sure to get to the edges of the tabs.

The hat should slide down onto the Snowman's head. Twist the hat into position until the 'x' allows the hat to slide on.

Press down firmly on the hat to get it to stay securely on the head.

Snip small tassels in both ends of the scarf.

Glue on eyes, mouth buttons and paper buttons down the front.
Start from the front with the scarf. Find the center and wrap it to the back.

Tie one knot into the scarf at the back of the Snowman's neck.

Bring one of the ends of the scarf back to the front. Put a small amount of glue onto the front shoulder and glue the scarf down to keep it in the front.

If the scarf is too long, trip it to the desired length. You will need to cut tassels in the ends again if you trim it.

Here is your completed snowman. As with all of these characters, there are many ways that you can personalize him.

Make him a felt beanie rather than a top hat. Give him ear muffs, put felt mittens on him or give him google eyes. Make him smaller and fatter or taller and thinner by changing paper sizes.

The snowman is a perfect craft to do with classrooms during the long winter months. Be creative, original and HAVE FUN!

The Bunny

The Bunny

MATERIALS

	Color	Paper
Body (2 chompers)	Pink	6" X 9"
Head (2 chompers)	Pink	4 1/2" X 6"
Mouth (x1), Inside of Ears (x2)	Red / Dk.Pink	Use patterns
Ears, Arms, Legs (x2 each)	Pink	Use pattern
Eyes (x2)	Outside white / inside black	Use pattern
Paw Pads	Dk. Pink	Use patterns
Teeth	White	Use patterns
Whiskers	White	Use paper strips or pipe cleaners
Other Materials	Tacky Glue, scissors, pink pompom	cotton ball for tail, pipe cleaners for whiskers

GETTING STARTED

Begin by getting all of your pieces traced, cut and folded. Use the directions for 'The Chomper' on **PAGES 9-15** to make the head and body parts.

Pattern pieces for the rest of your character are included in the back of the book on **PAGES 124-125.**

As you know, Easter Bunnies come in a variety of colors and sizes. I chose pink for the model, but go ahead and make him brown, yellow, white, black or even blue. When I used to make them with students, I would let them choose the color they wanted and we would have a rainbow of Bunnies hanging from our ceiling. He doesn't need to be an Easter Bunny...he can be just a plain old bunny to go along with a great book or project that you are doing.

Have fun making your Bunny as large, small, fat or as colorful as you wish. He can carry an Easter Basket or hold onto an Easter Egg that has a piece of writing attached to it. If you are studying animal groups or have the first book in the Paper Fold Creations focusing on Animal Groups, make the Bunny in place of the Tiger as your mammal.

MAKING AND ATTACHING THE HEAD AND BODY

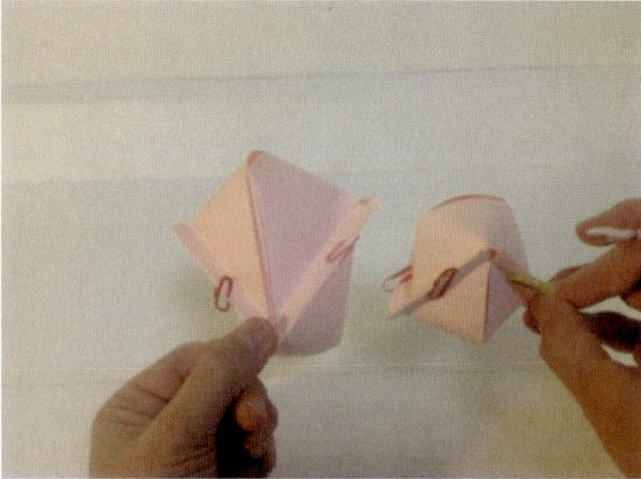

Using the directions on **PAGES 9-14** make the head and the body of the Bunny.

Attach the head to the body using the directions on **PAGES 15-16**.

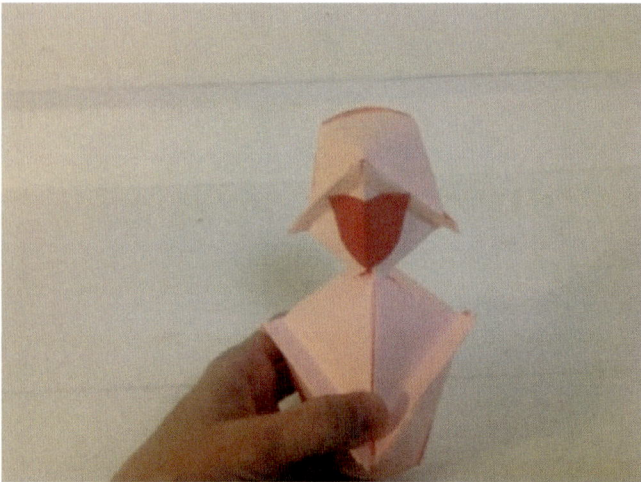

Glue the red mouth piece to the front of the Bunny's face as shown.

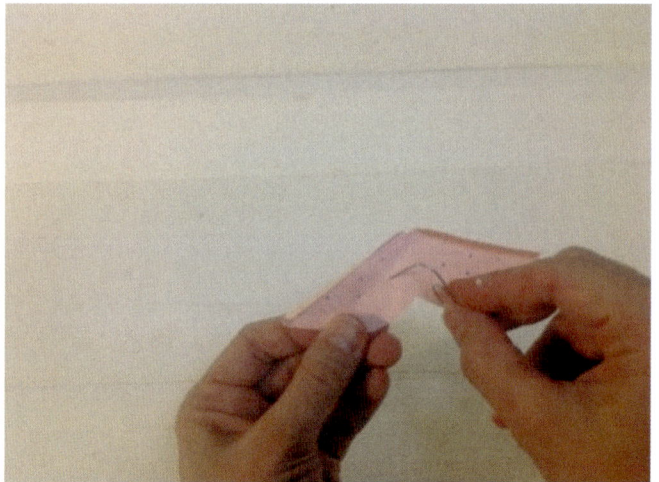

Using a paperclip, poke three holes in each cheek.
I recommend skipping these next steps with children and having them draw whiskers on with marker instead.

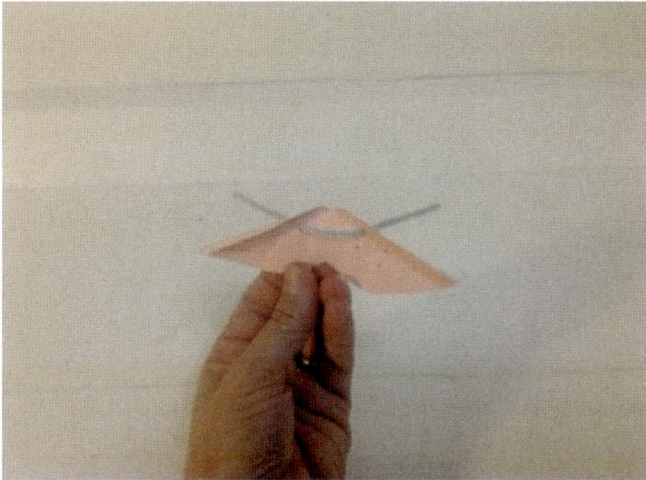

Thread one of the pipe cleaners front, back front. This is the top whisker.

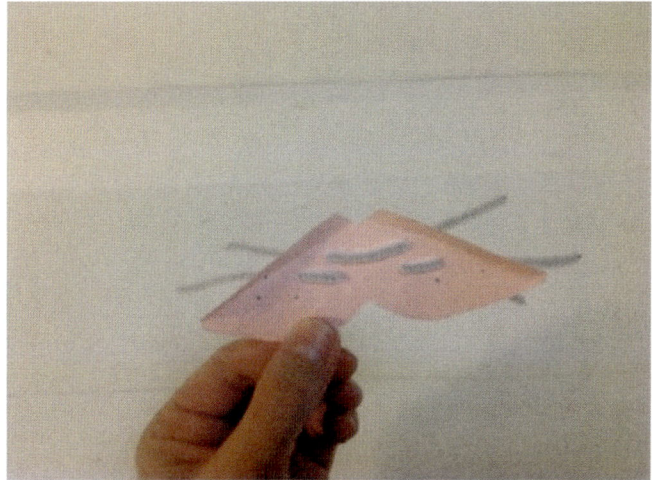

Thread the other two pipe cleaners, one for each cheek. On one cheek, go front, back, front with one whisker. Do the same with the last whisker.

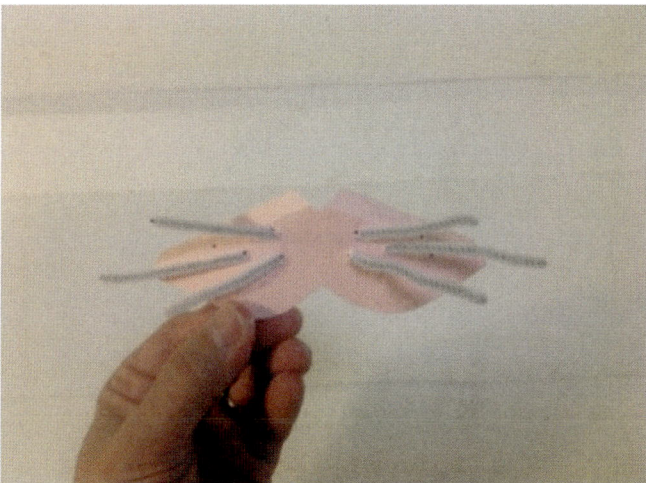

From the front the Bunny face and whiskers will look like this.

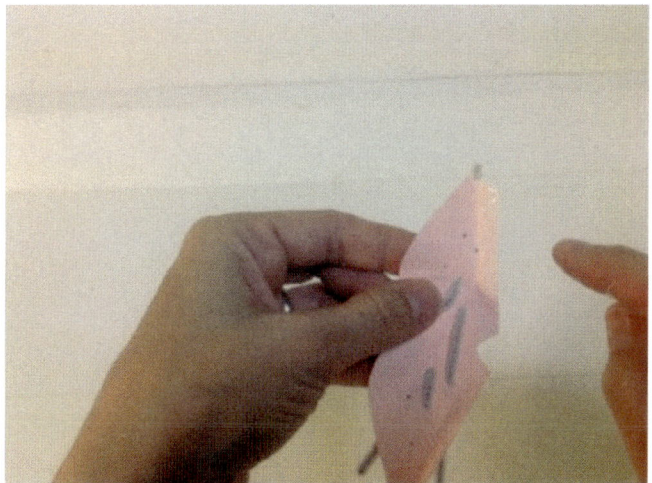

Fold down the edges of the face piece and apply glue to the inside edges.

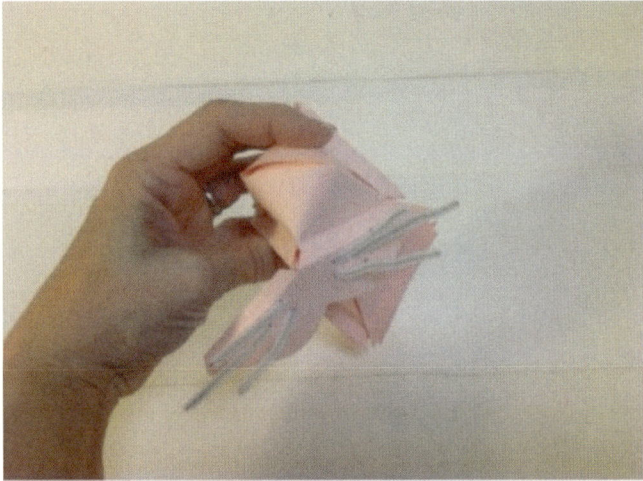

Glue the face tab to the upward pointing 'v' on the face.

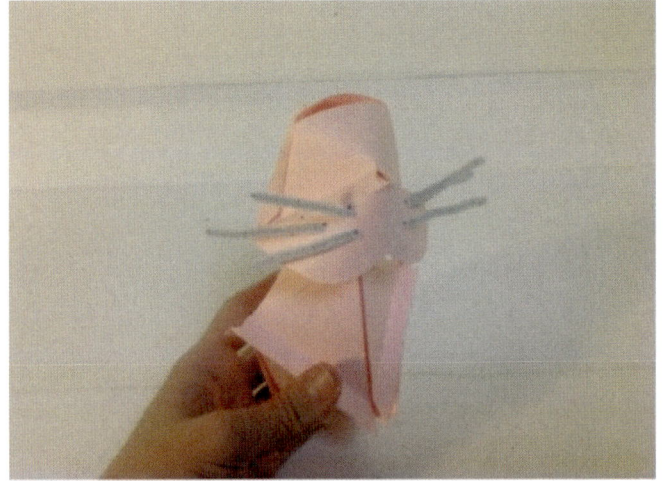

Wrap the face piece around to the other side and glue down.

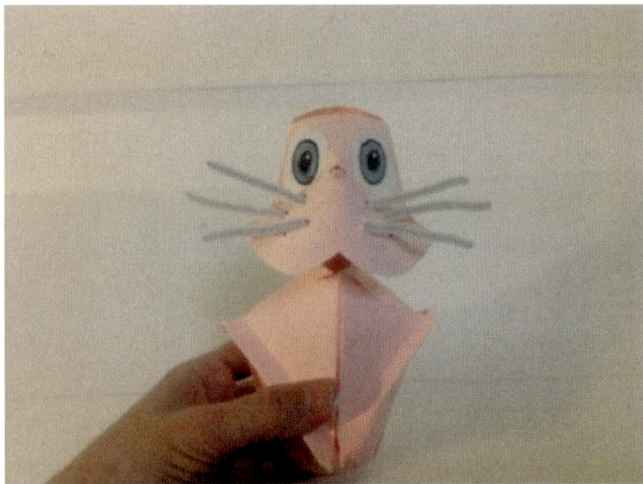

This bunny has green eyes, but you can make them whatever color you like.

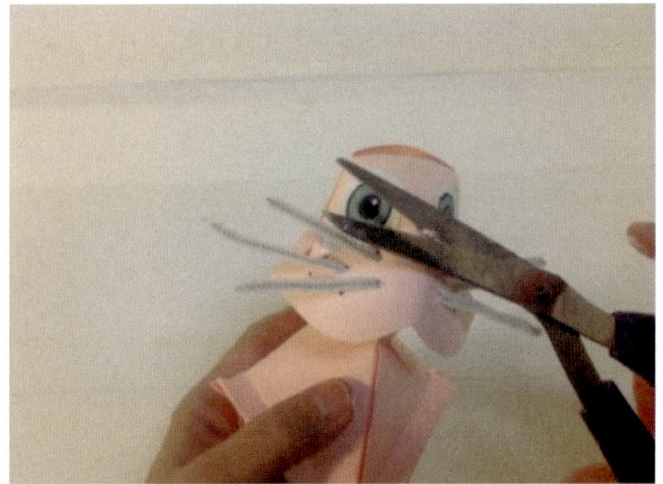

Snip the tip of the nose off to have a flat space to glue on the pompom nose.

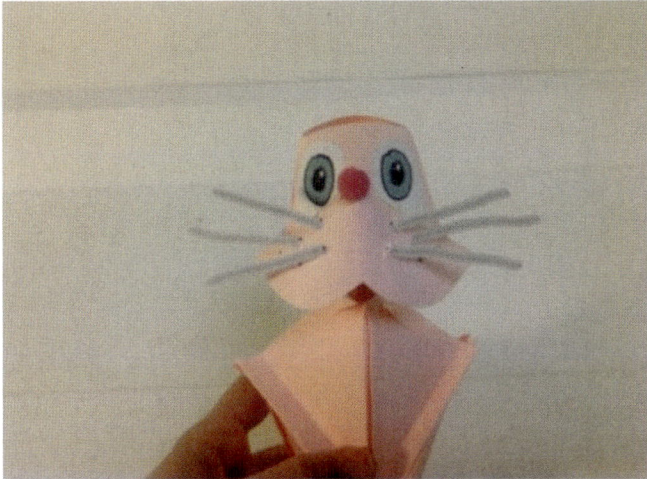

Using tacky glue or a hot glue gun, glue the pompom nose onto the face.

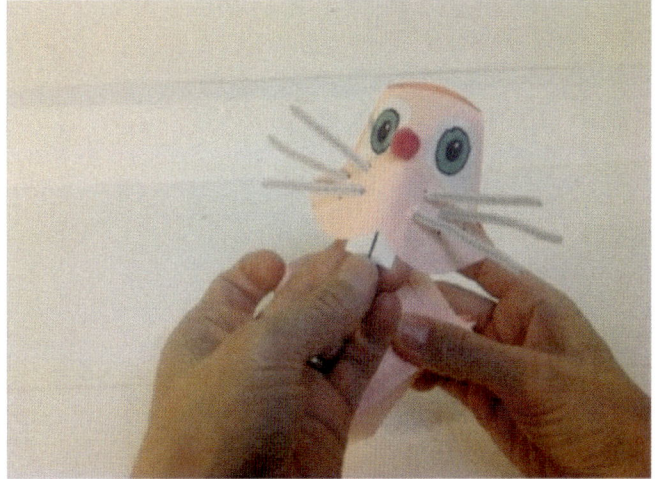

Glue the Bunny's teeth to the inside of the face piece.

Glue the insides of the Bunny ears onto the outer ears.

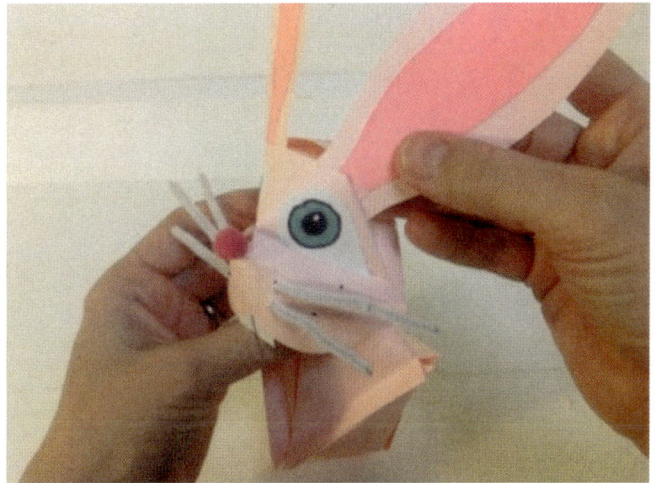

Put glue on the bottom of the ears and insert them into the seam on the top of the head as shown. How you position your Bunny's ears will give it different personalities.

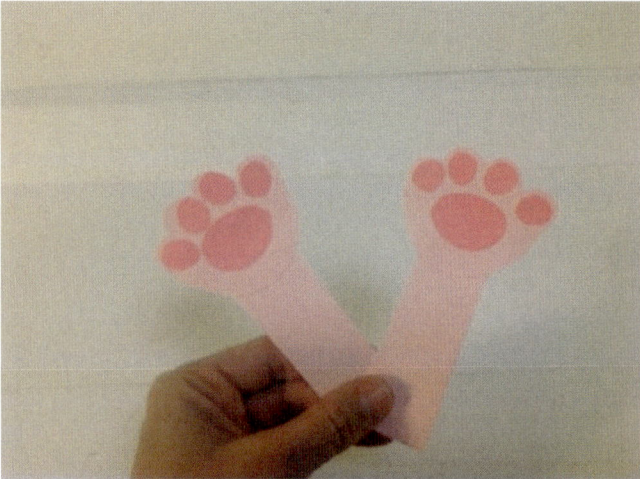

Glue the pads onto the paws as shown and glue the hands to the arms.

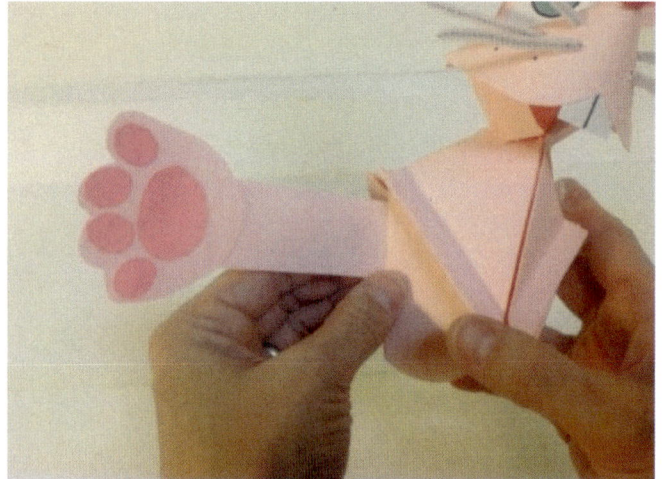

Attach the arms to the body as shown on **PAGE 16.** Bend at the elbows.

Bend the ears forward a bit so they don't stick straight up.

You're almost finished...you just need the legs and tail!

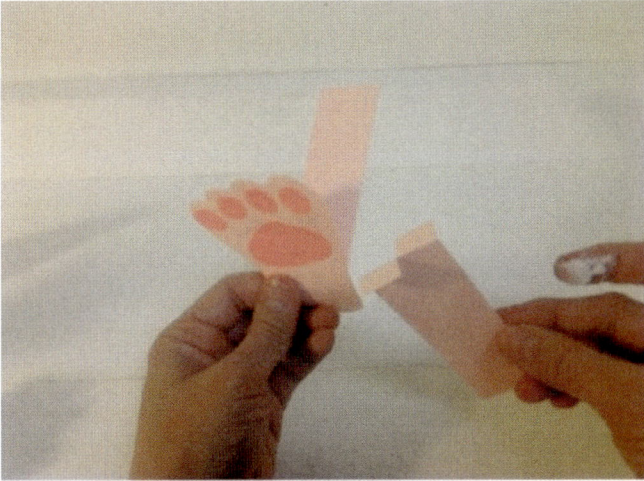

Glue the pads to the feet as shown in the picture. Attach the feet to the legs using the directions on **PAGE 17**.

Attach the legs using the directions on **PAGE 17**.

Glue on a cotton ball for the tail!

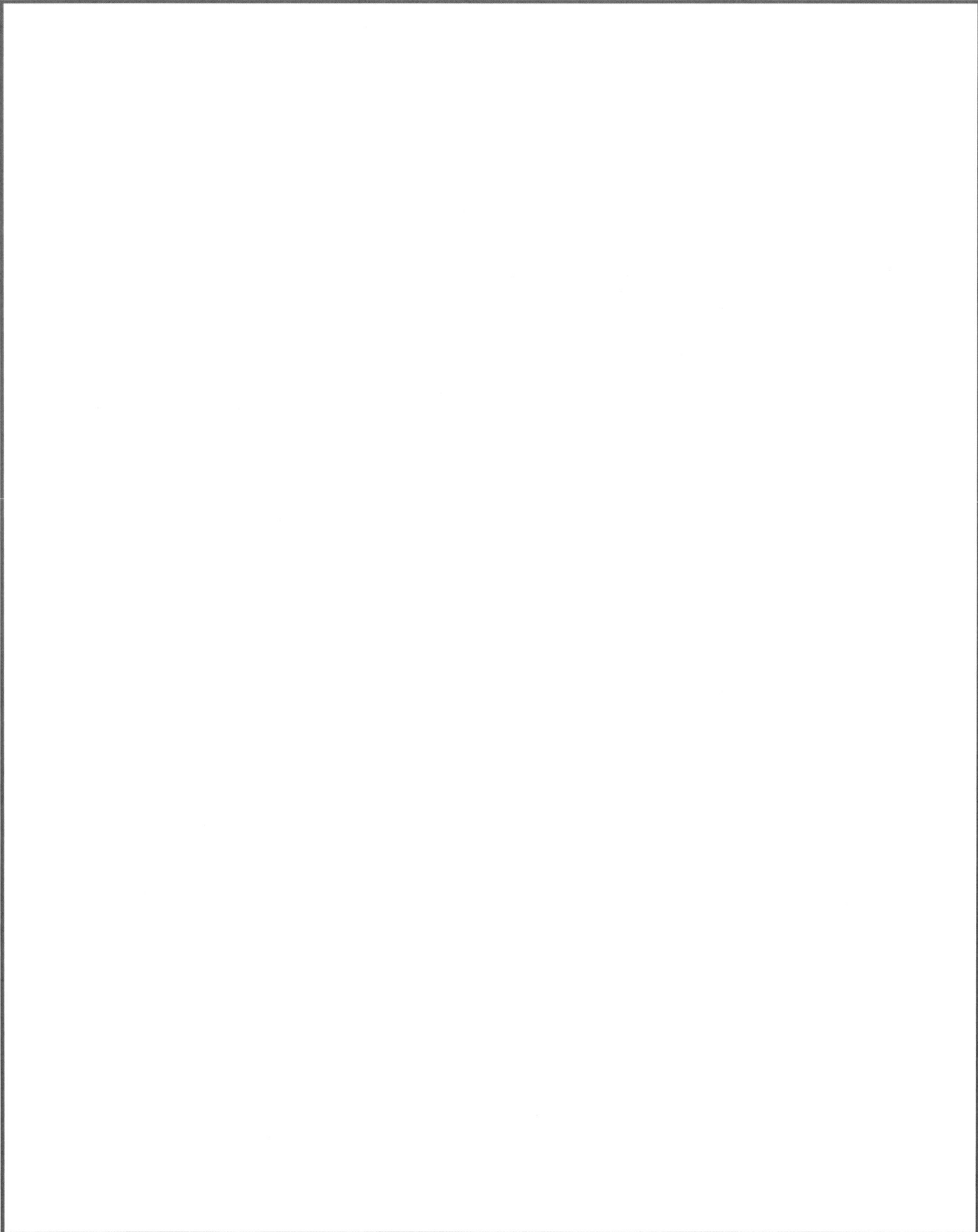

Pattern Pieces

Scarecrow Pattern Pieces

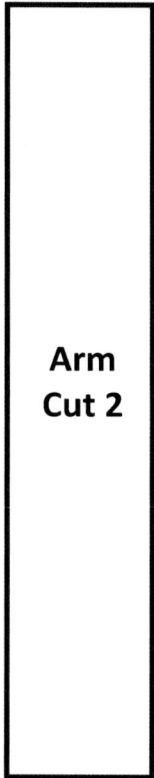

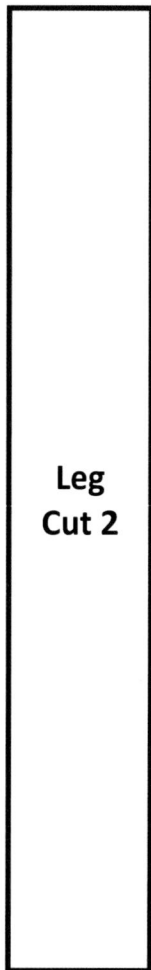

**Arm
Cut 2**

**Leg
Cut 2**

**Eyes
Cut 1 Each**

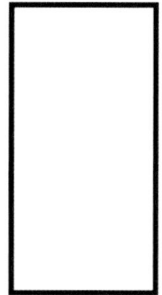

**Head / Body
Connector
Cut 2**

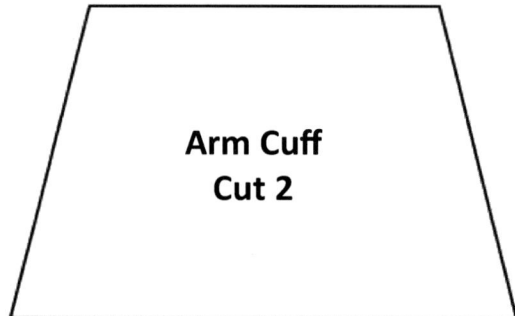

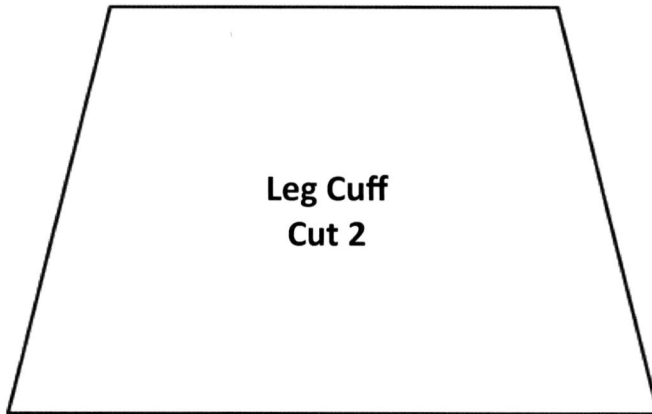

**Arm Cuff
Cut 2**

**Leg Cuff
Cut 2**

Bottom of Hat
Cut 1

Top of Hat
Cut 1

Rectangle for Hat
Cut 1

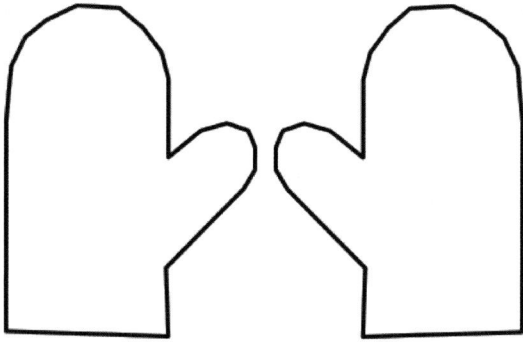

Hands
Cut 2

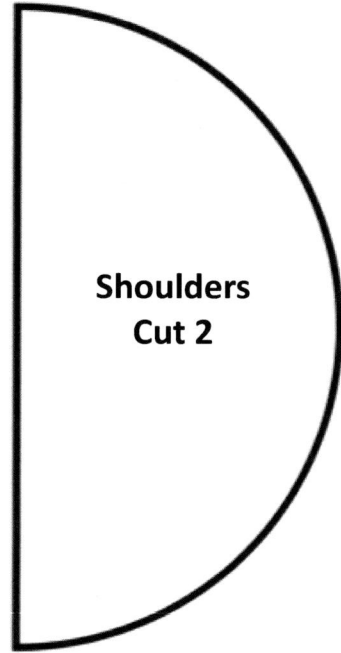

Shoulders
Cut 2

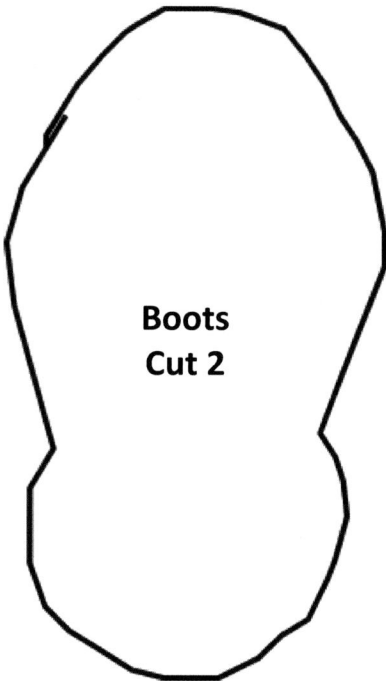

Boots
Cut 2

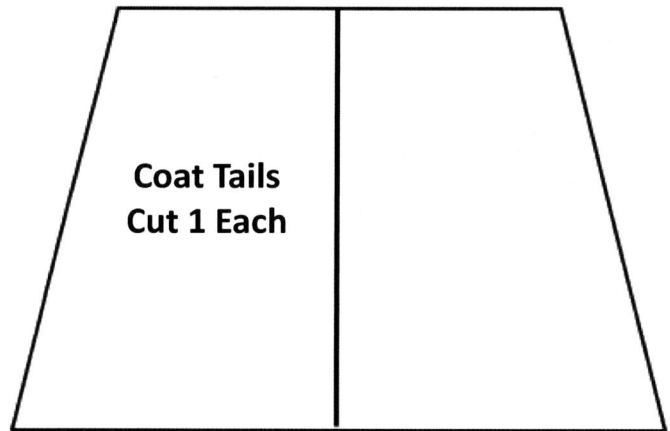

Coat Tails
Cut 1 Each

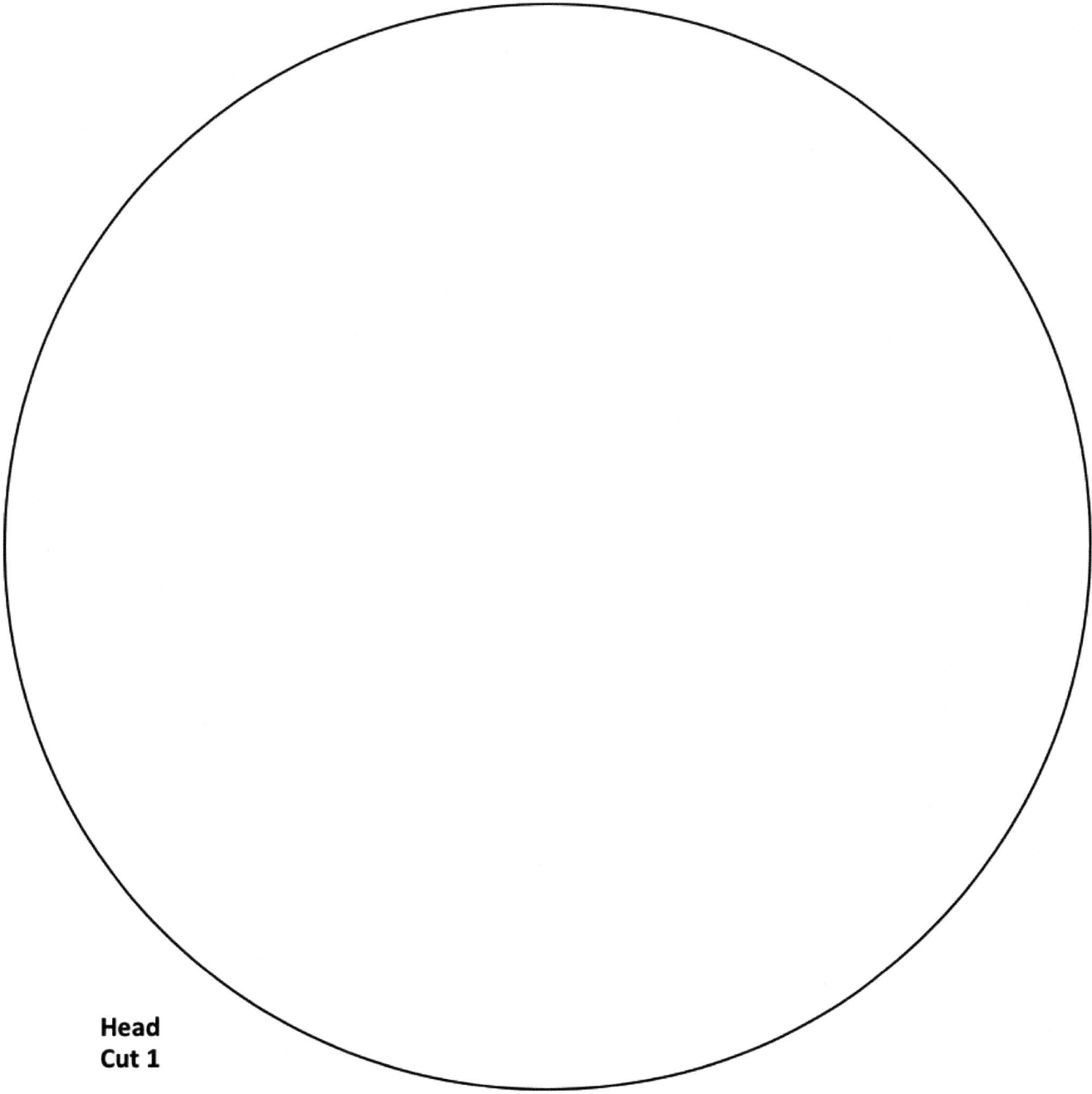

**Head
Cut 1**

**Jacket Lapel
Cut 2**

Witch Pattern Pieces

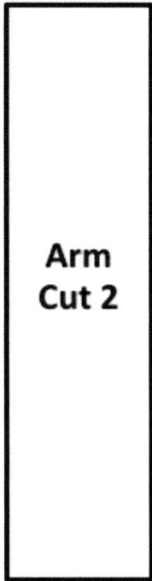

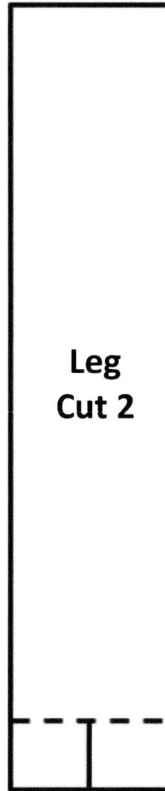

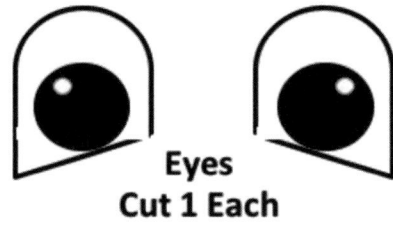

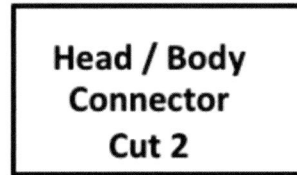

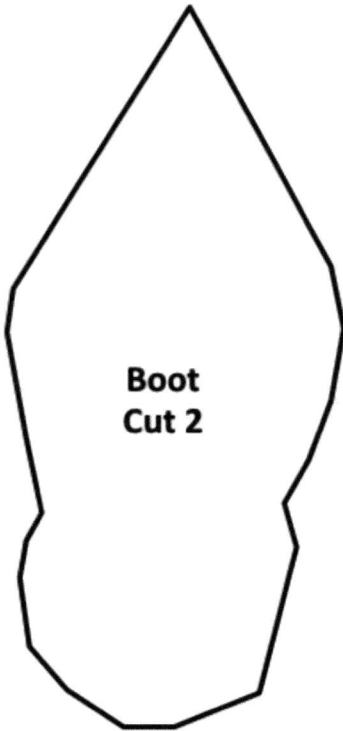

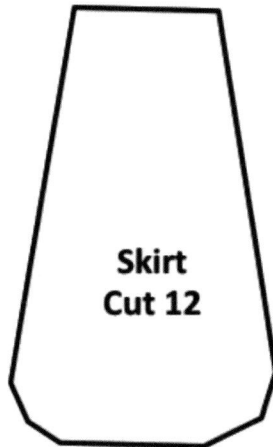

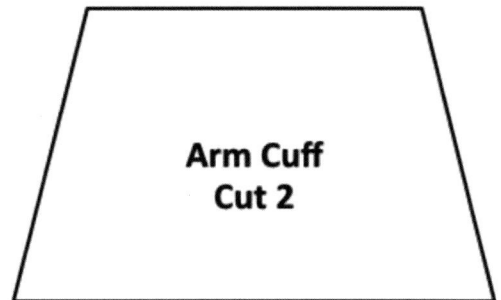

Arm
Cut 2

Leg
Cut 2

Eyes
Cut 1 Each

Head / Body
Connector
Cut 2

Boot
Cut 2

Arm Cuff
Cut 2

Skirt
Cut 12

Cone For Nose
Cut 1

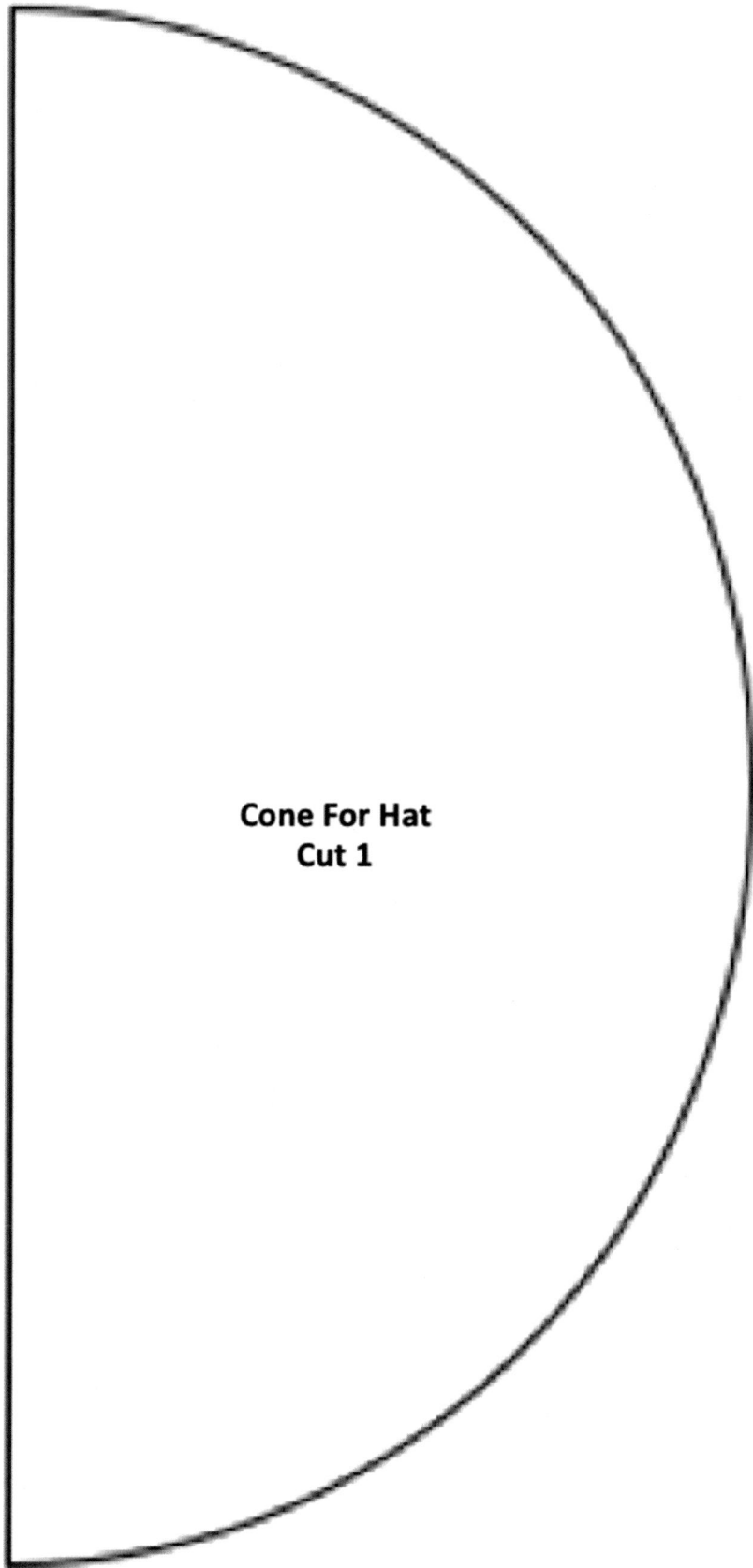

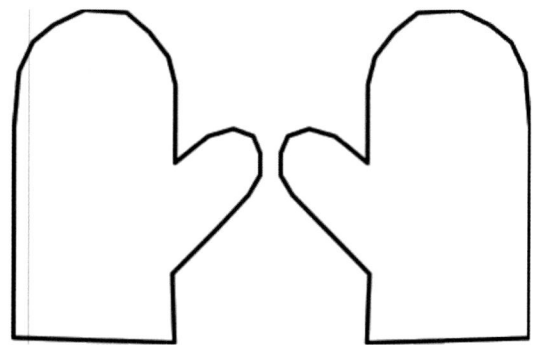

Cone For Hat
Cut 1

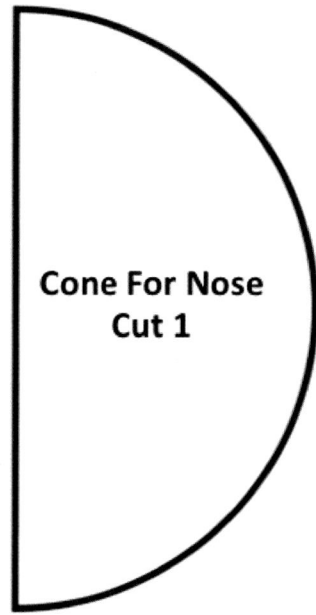

Hands
Cut 2

Hat Rim
Cut 1

Hat Strip
You choose color
Cut 1

Top of Boot
Cut 2

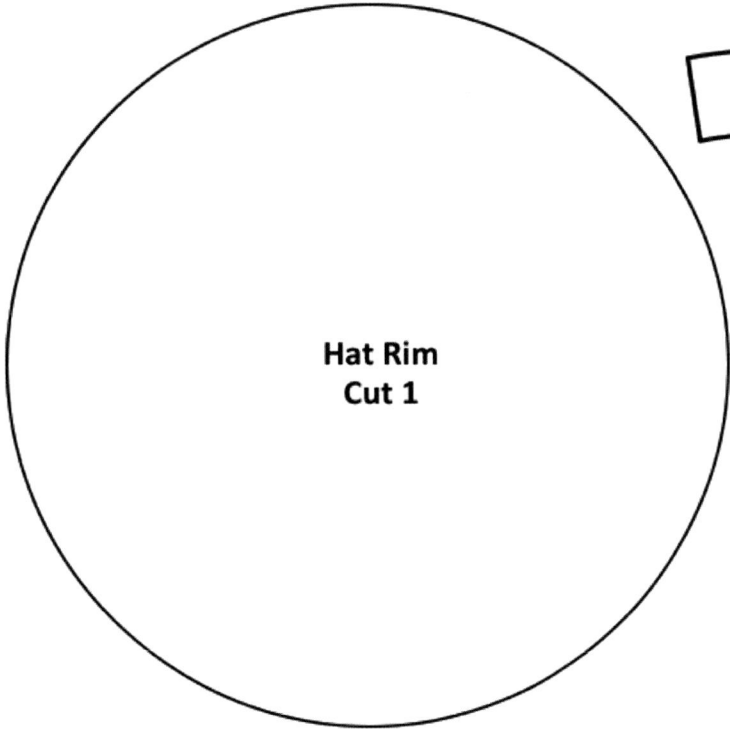

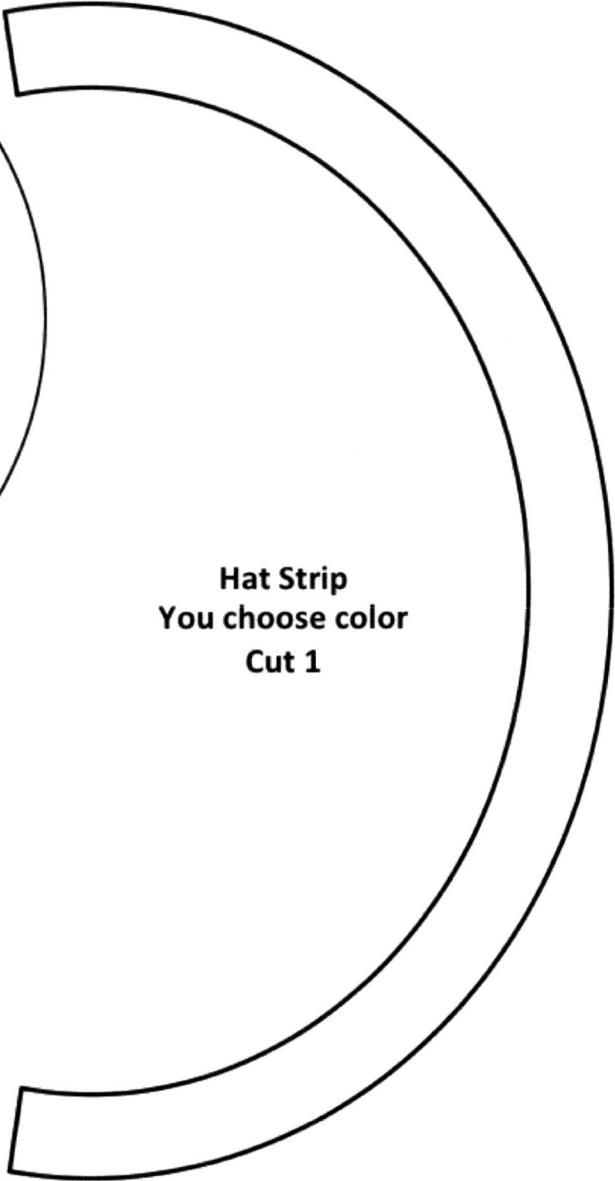

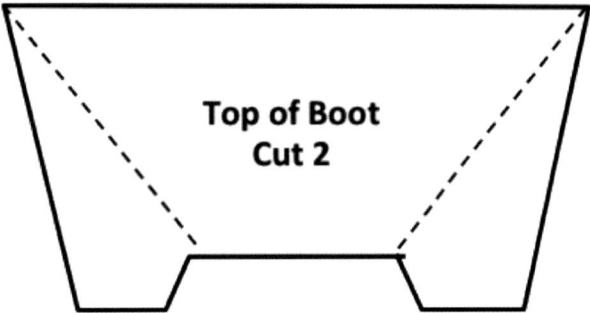

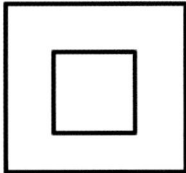

Hat Buckle
Cut 1

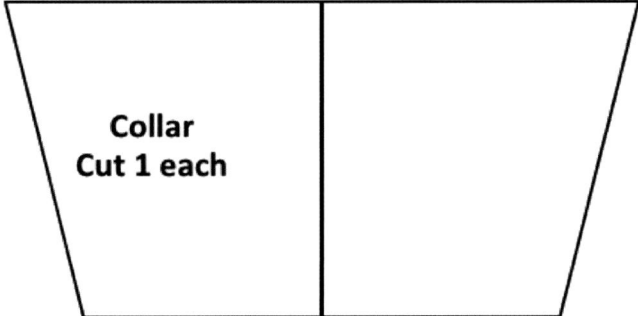

Collar
Cut 1 each

Turkey Pattern Pieces

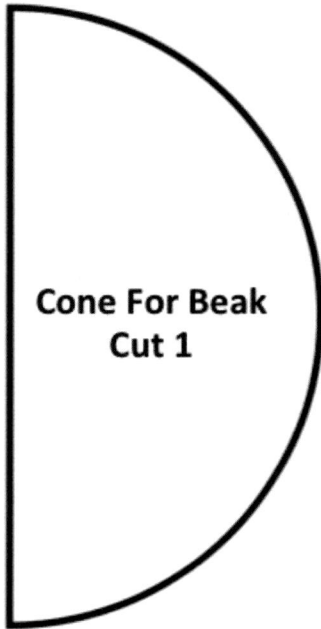

Cone For Beak
Cut 1

Eyes
Cut 1 Each

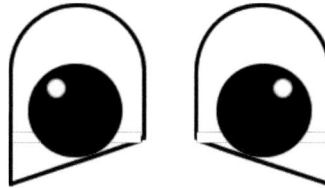

Head / Body
Connector
Cut 2

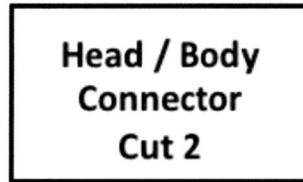

Alternate / Easier Tail
Cut 1

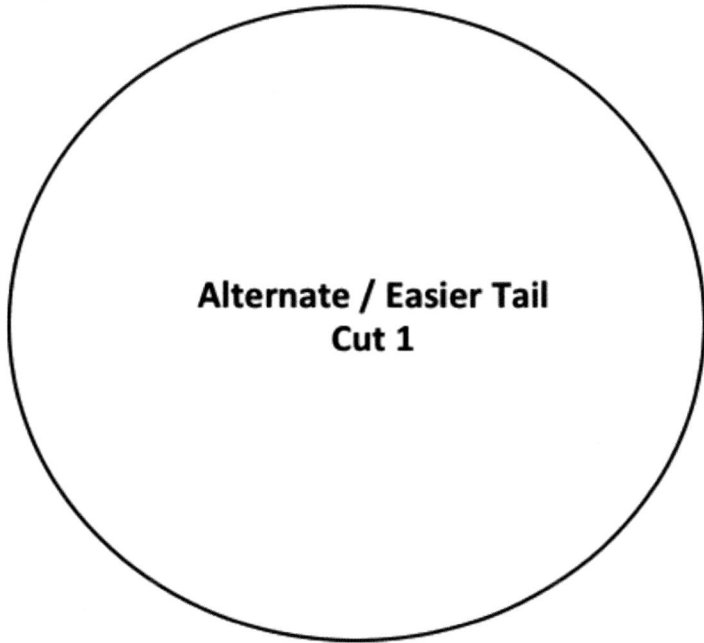

Hat Buckle
Cut 1

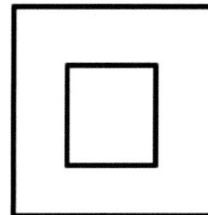

Feathers for Alternate Tail
Cut 10 of each color

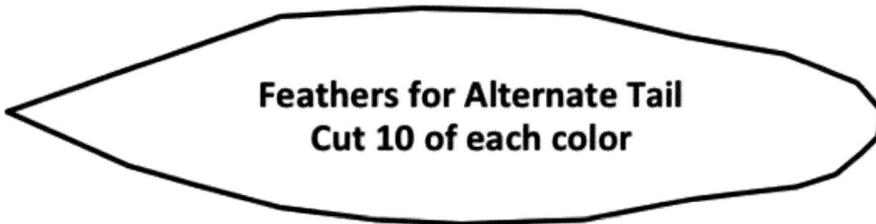

Bottom of Hat
Cut 1

Top of Hat
Cut 1

Rectangle for Hat
Cut 1

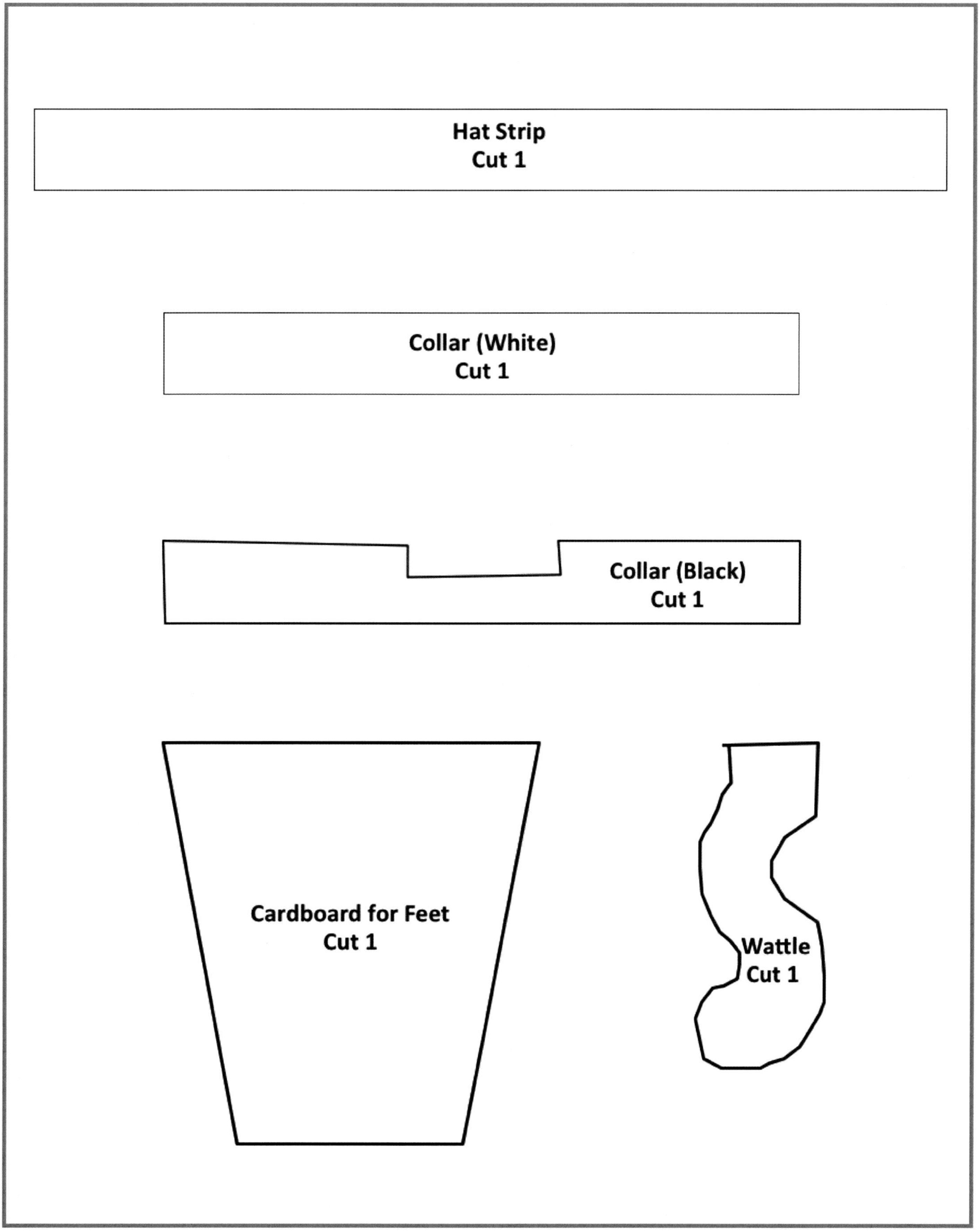

Hat Strip
Cut 1

Collar (White)
Cut 1

Collar (Black)
Cut 1

Cardboard for Feet
Cut 1

Wattle
Cut 1

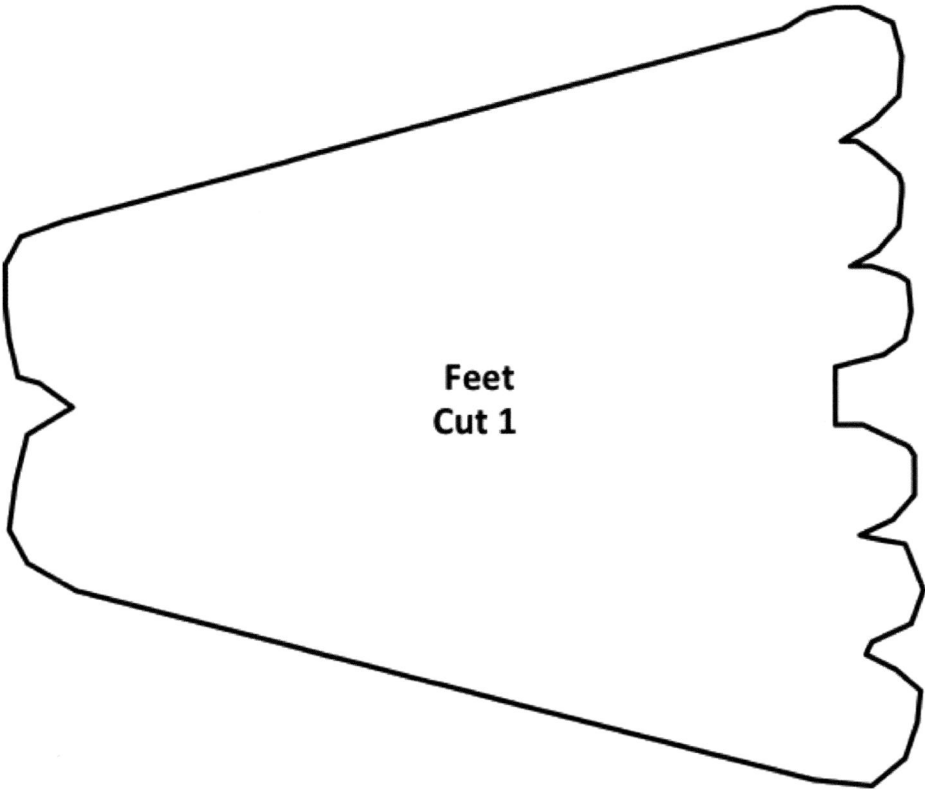

Feet
Cut 1

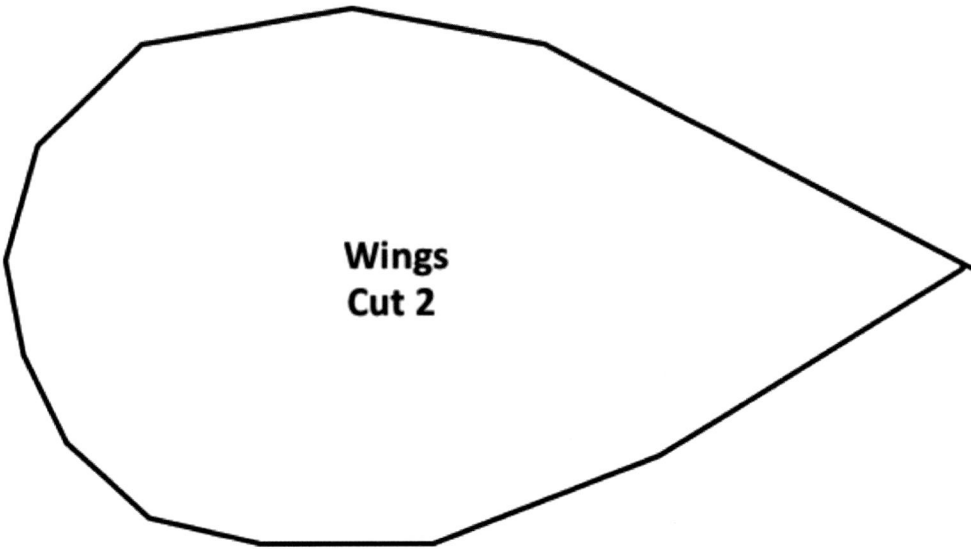

Wings
Cut 2

Santa Pattern Pieces

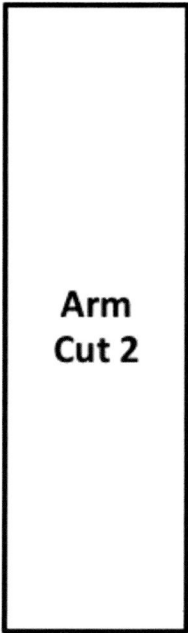

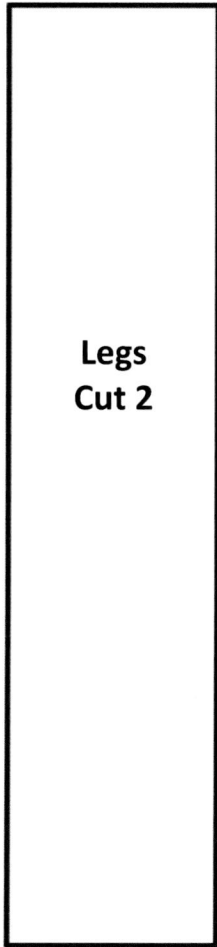

Arm
Cut 2

Legs
Cut 2

Eyes
Cut 1 Each

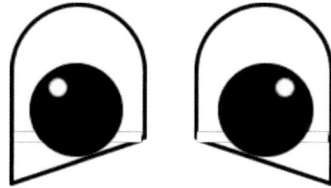

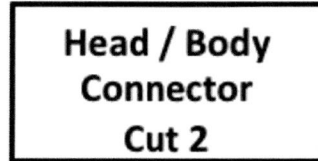

Head / Body
Connector
Cut 2

Leg/Boot
Connector
Cut 2

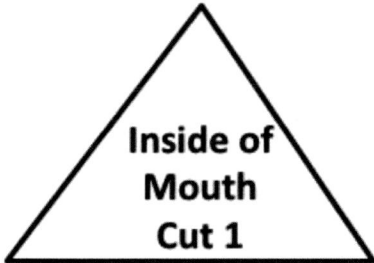

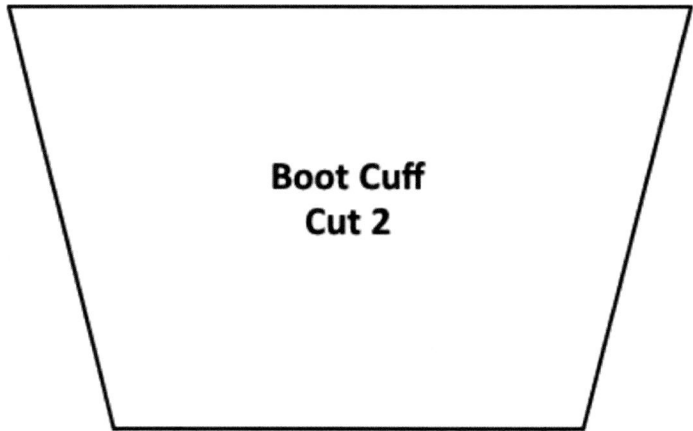

Inside of
Mouth
Cut 1

Boot Cuff
Cut 2

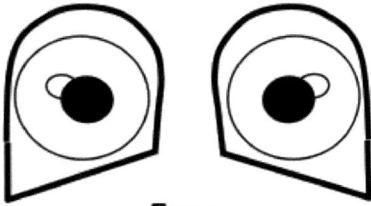

Eyes
You choose color
Cut 1 Each

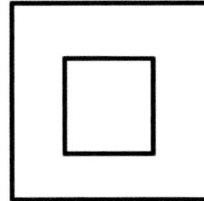

Belt Buckle
Cut 1

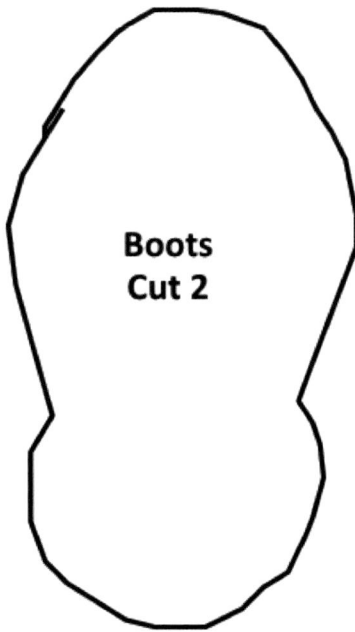

Boots
Cut 2

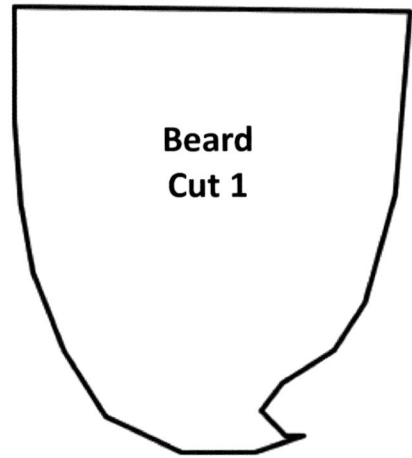

Beard
Cut 1

Mustache
Cut 1

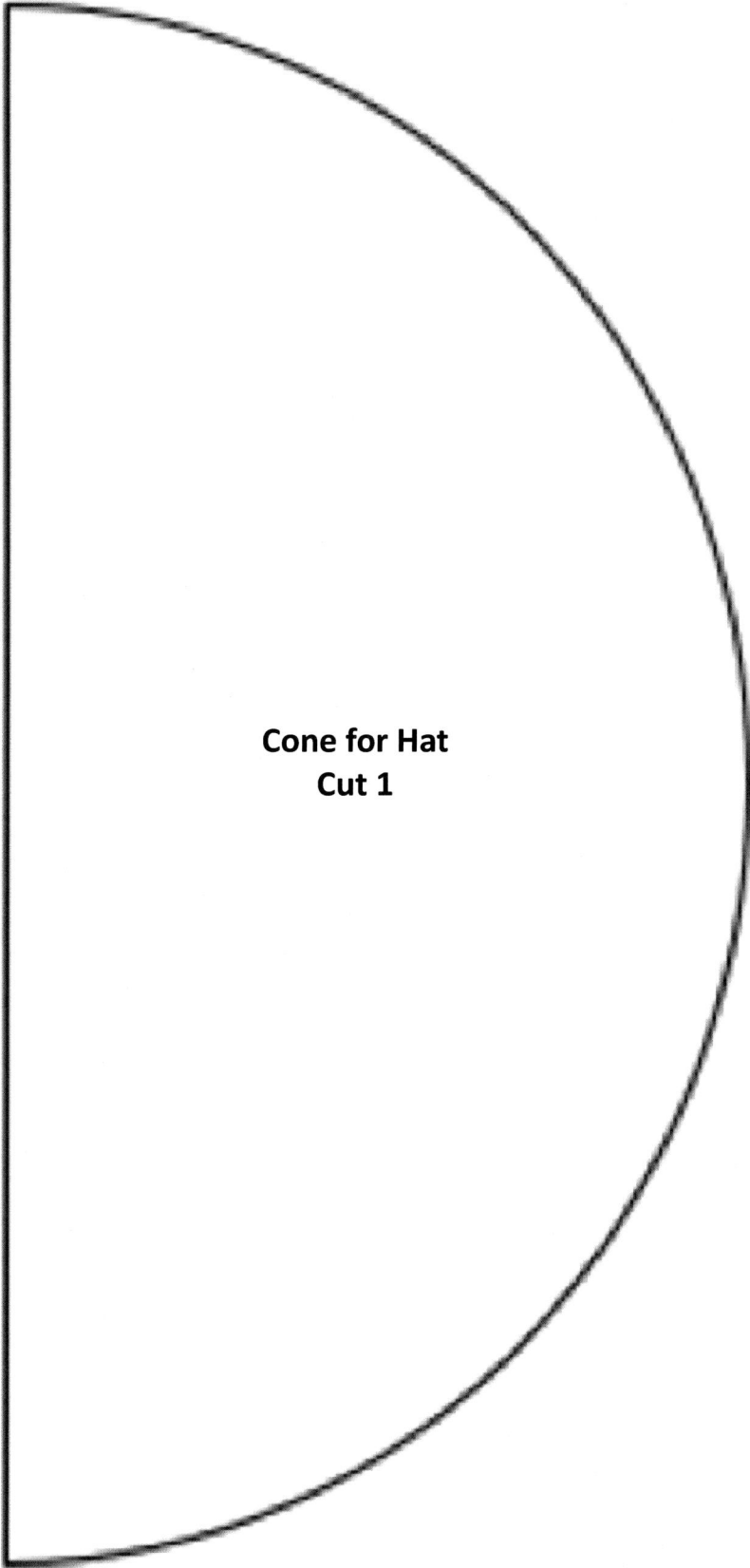

Cone for Hat
Cut 1

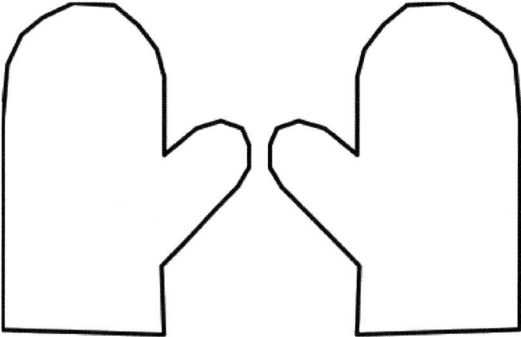

Hands
Cut 2

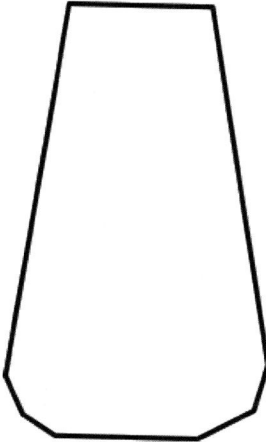

Jacket
Cut 11

Snowman Pattern Pieces

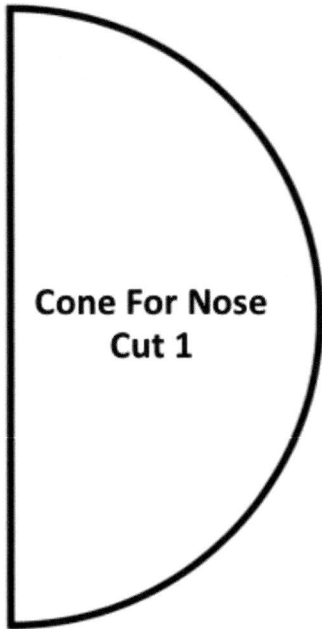

Cone For Nose
Cut 1

Eyes
Cut 1 Each

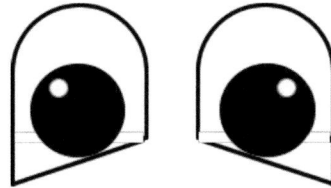

Head / Body
Connector
Cut 2

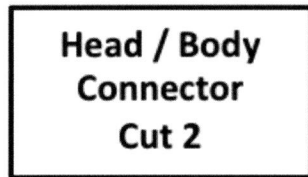

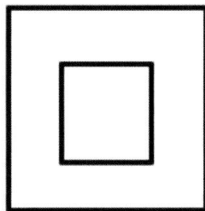

Hat Buckle
Cut 1

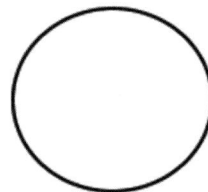

Buttons
(For front, eyes or
mouth)
Cut as needed

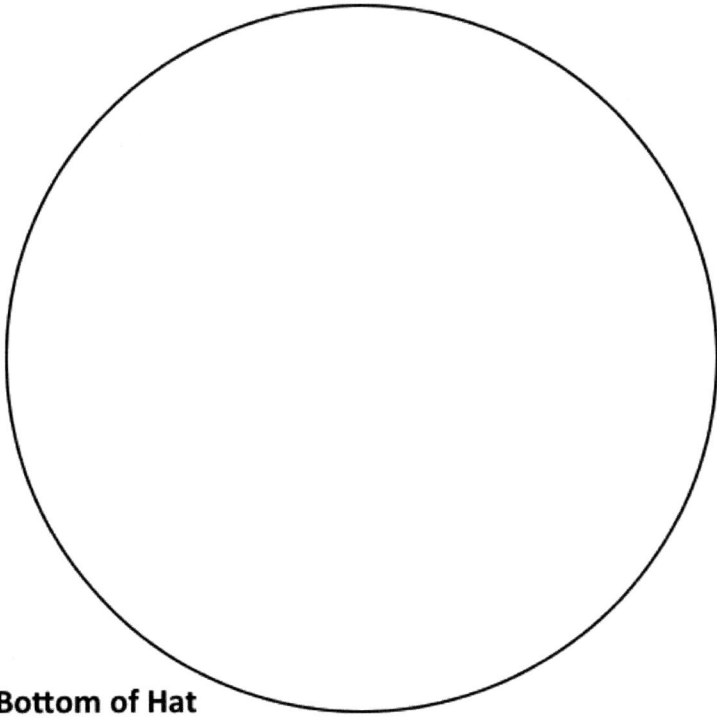

Bottom of Hat
Cut 1

Rectangle for Hat
Cut 1

Hat Strip
Cut 1

Bunny Pattern Pieces

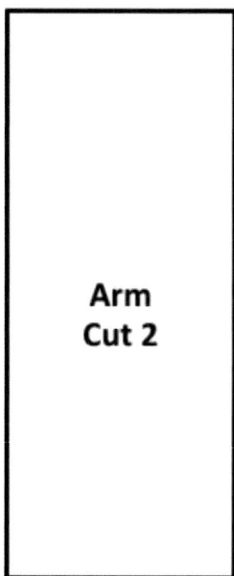

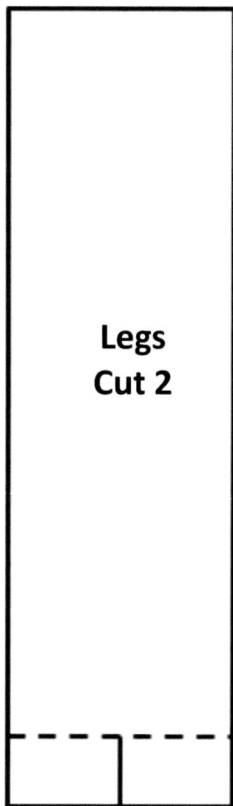

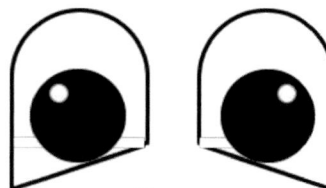

**Arm
Cut 2**

**Legs
Cut 2**

**Eyes
Cut 1 Each**

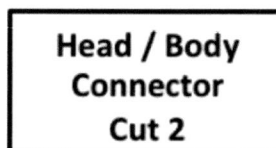

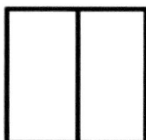

**Head / Body
Connector
Cut 2**

**Inside of
Mouth
Cut 1**

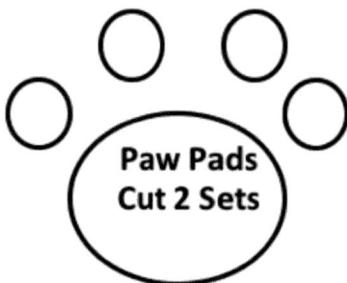

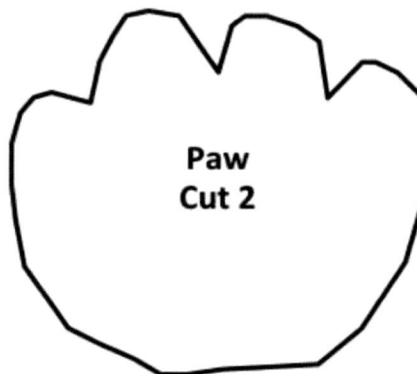

**Teeth
Cut 1 set**

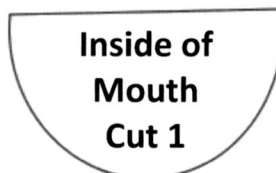

**Paw Pads
Cut 2 Sets**

**Paw
Cut 2**

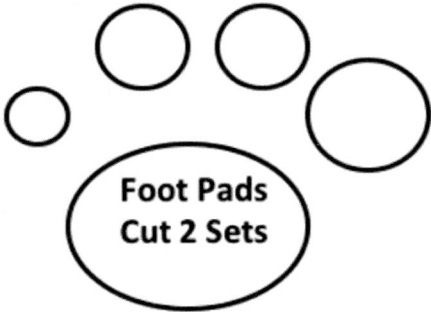

**Foot Pads
Cut 2 Sets**

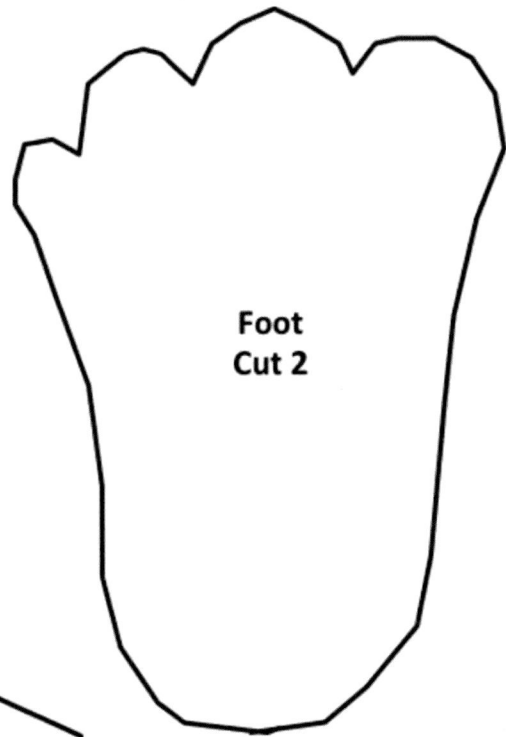

**Foot
Cut 2**

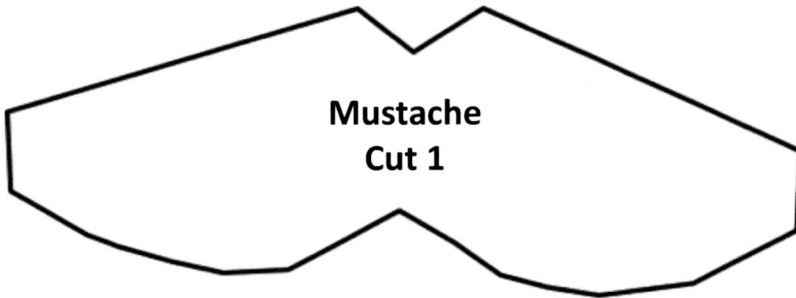

**Mustache
Cut 1**

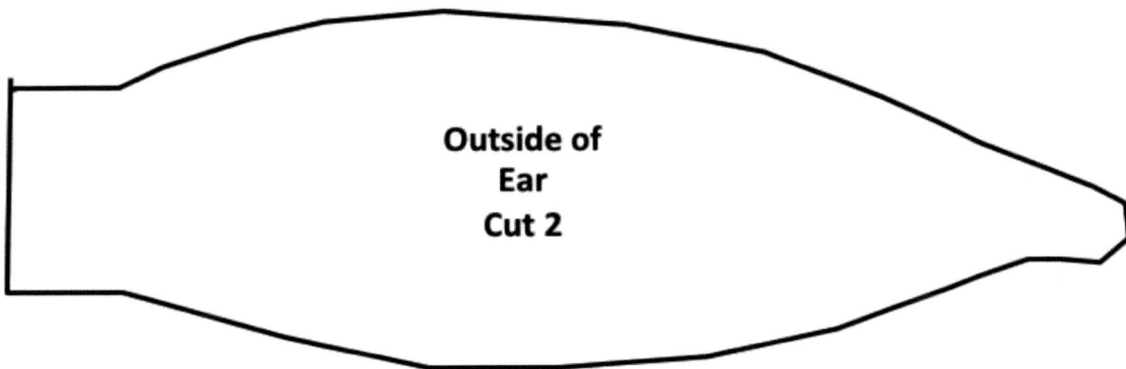

**Outside of
Ear
Cut 2**

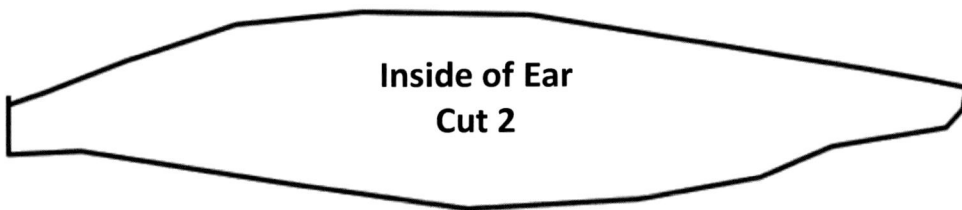

**Inside of Ear
Cut 2**

GLOSSARY

accordian fold	Also called the 'fan fold'; fold paper back and forth like the bellows of an accordion
center fold	The fold in the very center of the pattern piece
cone	A 3D geometric shape that tapers from a circular base to a point
connector piece	The piece used to connect the head to the body
crosshatch	To shade an area with intersecting sets of parallel lines
cuff	The material at the end of a sleeve or pant leg that is turned or sewn back
degrees, 180	An angle measurement; in this case 180 degrees is turning your paper upside down
fibrous	Characterized by having lots of fibers; fibrous paper is rougher and tears more easily
foil paper	Paper that has a metallic look to it
hexagon	A 2D shape (plane figure) with six straight sides and angles

horizontally	A line that goes side to side (East to West) rather than up and down (vertically or North to South)
lapel	The part on each side of a jacket just below the collar that is folded back on either side of the front opening
notch	An indentation or gap on the edge or surface of an object
tagboard	A sturdy cardboard used for making posters, labels and other items
Tru-Ray	Brand of construction paper
wattle	The colored, fleshy piece of skin that hangs from the neck of birds like turkeys and chickens

INDEX

ABOUT THE AUTHOR

Delia Lefebvre has been an elementary school teacher for more than twenty years, but started making these creations when she was a child herself. The characters have evolved over time and are constantly being added to. Many of these creatures have been made with classrooms of children over the years and have enhanced many lessons and units of study.

Delia lives in Vermont with her husband and two children. As well as being a full-time parent and teacher, she is also an artist who dabbles in paper crafts, painting, wood carving, knitting, crocheting, drawing, stained glass and clay work. She has more Paper Fold Creation books in the works, as well as some children's picture books.

Whenever there is time, she tries to enjoy the beautiful Northeast Kingdom of Vermont by hiking, kayaking, snowshoeing, snowboarding, mountain biking and gardening.

Coming Soon!

Knights and Dragons

This third book in the Paper Fold Creations series includes directions, patterns and photos to make:

The Knight
The Dragon
The Princess
The King
The Jester
The Wizard

Made in the USA
Las Vegas, NV
17 October 2021